THE FIRST
SEATTLE CATALOGUE

THE FIRST
SEATTLE
CATALOGUE

All the appurtenances
of a civilized,
amusing, and comfortable life

BY COLIN DOBSON AND KATHLEEN CAIN

Ensemble Publications

Photography by Robbie Milne and Todd Pearson.
Graphics by Total Print Services Inc.
Chapter illustrations by Wilkins & Peterson.
Cover: Painting by Gertrude Pacific.
       Arranged by the Linda Farris Gallery.
       Graphic design by Anne Traver.

Editor: Heather Prittie
Production Staff: Dorinda Gier
                 Vicki Kapetan
                 Rita McGee
                 Sally Quarles
                 Michele Stonebraker

Ensemble Publications also wishes to acknowledge
the advice and support extended by many
individuals, and to thank in particular Michael
Fleming, Lorna Gardner, Michael Levin, Howard
Wollner, Patricia Silverman, Carol Keaton, Marcia
Johnson, Francesca St. Clair, Daryl Hume, Marjorie
Siegel, and Susan Johnston whose efforts and
insights were especially valuable.

ISBN 0-920770-02-9
ISSN 0195-9166
Printed in Canada.

Contents

Introduction

It seems like everybody's talking about Seattle these days.

Seattle used to be the Great Escape. People would come here to get away from the noise and pollution of the big cities, because it was the next best thing to going to the woods. But nobody really stayed here, except for the tenacious natives who, having been born in Seattle, didn't know any better anyway. After basking in our spectacular scenery, the others would return to their cities on the East Coast or California... cities that offered the excitement and cultural stimulation that this fresh air mecca on Puget Sound lacked.

In the past ten years, especially in the past five, the situation has changed dramatically. No longer the Great Escape, Seattle is now the Great Destination. People are abandoning the crowded, congested big centers in favor of living here, because Seattle now offers all the sophistication of those places and very few of the disadvantages.

The First Seattle Catalogue is our response to that change. Herein, we have collected many of the reasons why Seattle is so compelling...the most civilized city in the United States.

Seattle has been discovered by the rest of the country. Recent articles in Time, Atlantic, Harper's and other national magazines rhapsodically enumerate the attractions of Seattle and the Pacific Northwest, pointing out the various cultural and scenic wonders with a kind of surprised awe, as if these phenomena had sprung up overnight like some peculiar toadstool. But the people who live here have known all that for a long time. They're the ones who've made this the place with the largest number of successful theatre companies outside New York City. They're the ones who attend the Opera, follow the thriving sports scene, patronize the shops and galleries, visit the parks, and dine in the restaurants that have all contributed so much to Seattle's famous "livability". The First Seattle Catalogue was intended, first and foremost, for those people. But where city residents flock, savvy visitors soon follow. For them, The First Seattle Catalogue provides the inside track...a convenient, easy-to-use and entertaining overview of the city's most worthwhile places.

The people who created The First Seattle Catalogue know the city intimately. They spent many hours seeking out and selecting the best, the unusual, the most intriguing, professional and well-loved places in town. You'll find many of your old favorites here, in company with lots of exciting discoveries. Even the most established natives will be amazed at how many places there are in Seattle that they haven't yet experienced. The selection here reflects the ethnic diversity of the city, its many free attractions, the sophisticated dining and entertainment scene, and much more.

The establishments included in this book have been carefully selected by the publisher and his staff. Each place was chosen for its singluar contribution to city-life, and each in turn contributed to the production costs in precise proportion to the space utilized. Without their support, a book of this scope could not have been published; but because of it, The First Seattle Catalogue is able to present a classic, thorough portrait of the city we love.

We hope you enjoy The First Seattle Catalogue. We plan to produce a new one every other year, so that Seattleites and Seattle-watchers all over the country will always have something to talk about.

Sports

Photo: Historical Society of Seattle & King County

A friend of mine told me that the last time he visited Seattle, there was 6" of rain. In his room.

Wayne Cody

The Locker Room

525 PIKE STREET
682-8284
HOURS: MONDAY-FRIDAY 9:30-6:00
SATURDAY 10:00-5:00

The Locker Room is a sports store designed especially for fans. And without them, who'd make all the hoopla to drown out the grunts and groans of pain down there on the field? Yes, the fans definitely know where it's at, and so does the Locker Room . . . a very busy place in a city that takes such a huge interest in its home teams.

During the 1979 Sonics victory sweep, owner Terry Friedlander had line-ups to contend with. Whether your interest is basketball or soccer, football or baseball, you'll find the best things to wear or wave or carry around with you . . . all emblazoned with your favorite team's logo. There are caps, hats, shorts, socks, jerseys, jackets, jewelry, lamps, radios, buttons, ashtrays, watches, pennants, pens, pencils and that fine old American tradition, the bumper sticker. All the official professional teams and leagues are represented, as well as a good stock of items from major college teams too. With luck, your visit will coincide with one of the frequent player appearances. If you are any kind of fan at all, you'll come out sporting the colors of your team. Visa. Master Charge. American Express.

Seattle Supersonics

**419 OCCIDENTAL S.
SEATTLE
MAIL: CALL BOX 14102,
SEATTLE 98114
BUSINESS: 628-8400
TICKET: 628-8444
HOURS: MONDAY-
FRIDAY 9:00-5:00**

There's not much you can say about the best professional basketball team in the country that isn't already evident to a town where everyone is a devoted fan. The Seattle Supersonics are the World Champions, and if you care to collect opinions, they're going to be World Champions for a long time. At least to us. A young NBA franchise, the team was created in 1967, but they've been popular since day-one, always tops in home-game attendance records. This team is a phenomenon. It's hard to say whether Seattleites are such passionate supporters because the team is so good, or whether the Sonics 1979 victory was tipped by that awesome devotion. At any rate, it's a hot love affair, and last season's win was the peak of an energy that had been building for years. The move to the Kingdome has been a tremendous boost, too, accommodating even more fans to surpass those attendance scores. More space has translated into reduced ticket prices, ranging from $1.50 to $10.00 . . . the best deals in professional basketball. Senior citizens and students qualify for special breaks, and Sunday games feature ticket discounts as well. The Seattle Supersonics have it all . . . thrilling court wizardry, true blue fans, and ticket prices everyone can afford. You couldn't ask for more . . . except maybe a King Dog and a beer.

Super Jock 'n Jill

7210 GREENLAKE DRIVE N.
522-7711
HOURS: MONDAY-FRIDAY 10:00-7:00
SATURDAY 10:00-6:00
SUNDAY 12:00-4:00

Super Jock 'n Jill is the sole food of Greenlake's runners. This shop sells the best in running footwear and accessories. It's also a source of information and inspiration to those who brave the rain, bikes, dogs, rollerskaters and ducks to do their laps around Greenlake each day. The shop is actively involved in several races, like the Bonne Bell 10k, Red Brick Road Half Marathon and the yearly Seattle Marathon, and has hosted clinics and informal visits by running experts like Rod Dixon, Don Kardong and Frank Shorter. The inventory at Jock 'n Jill is very ample and includes warm-up suits, socks, shorts, shirts, tote bags, caps and accessories plus, of course, a stock of running shoes by all track and field's worthiest brands. The salespeople at Super Jock 'n Jill are runners and know their sport. Their experience and product knowledge ensures that each foot forward is your best.
Visa. Master Charge.

Roller Company

7208 EAST GREENLAKE DRIVE N.
523-9398
HOURS: SEVEN DAYS A WEEK 8:30-9:00
CLOSED ON RAINY DAYS

What they need across from Roller Company is a sign reading "Caution: Roller Crossing". This roller skate sales, rental and service shop is becoming so popular that this wouldn't be a bad idea. Owners Peter Buser and Todd Gale, figuring that the roller skating rage was much more than a flash in the pan, researched the sport at the best outlets in Los Angeles and came home to introduce the sport as only experts can. They carry a large inventory of skates for sale, as well as 300 rental pairs. A mere $2 buys an hour's worth of the best fun you've probably had in a long time. Don't worry if you haven't done it for years . . . advice is gladly given to the novice. Accessories include wrist, knee and elbow pads, T-shirts as well as a complete line of skate parts if your own pair needs a little work. Since they are located across from Greenlake, Seattle's most popular outdoor skating area, you couldn't ask for more.

R.E.I. Travel

1525 11TH AVENUE
SEATTLE, WASHINGTON 98122
322-7800
HOURS: MONDAY-FRIDAY 9:00-5:00
WEDNESDAY UNTIL 9:00

Photo: Dan Tobin

R.E.I. Adventure Travel provides vacations for those who want more than the usual week on the beach with all the other tourists. A special department of R.E.I. Co-op, it's a full-service travel agency that can help you with bookings and information for any trip, but its specialty is emphatically the unusual . . . guided excursions to the mountains of Nepal, the jungles of Bolivia, the ruins of Incan civilization in the Andes, Alaskan glaciers, and a wide range of participatory treks and voyages to the forests and rivers of our own Northwest. You'll learn survival techniques, facts about wilderness preservation and, since most of these exploration packages involve a range of challenging physical activities, you'll come back in wonderful shape. R.E.I. Adventure Travel offers a catalog full of such opportunities as . . . skiing, rafting, cycling, trekking, canoeing, backpacking and mountaineering, led by some of the most experienced travelers on earth. Not for the sedentary sort, R.E.I. Adventure Travel is in fact Seattle's most thorough center for unusually-oriented travel advice and arrangements.

REI Co-op

1525 - 11TH AVENUE
323-8333
HOURS: MONDAY & TUESDAY 9:30-6:00
WEDNESDAY- FRIDAY 9:30-9:00
SATURDAY 9:00-5:30
MAIL-ORDER
P.O. BOX C-88188
SEATTLE, WASHINGTON 98188

In a city full of backpacking and recreational equipment stores, REI has always held its own, due to a sure-fire combination of longevity, quality, selection and price. This outlet was started by a group of mountaineers in the 1930's (among them REI President Jim Whittaker, the first man ever to reach the peak of Mt. Everest) because they couldn't find what they needed. It has snowballed into the biggest outdoor co-op of its kind in the world . . . there are 800,000 members. REI has made its reputation by seeking out the best quality merchandise and offering it to members at a good saving. You don't have to be a member to shop at REI, but the 10% dividend makes it worth your while. Mountaineering equipment isn't the only thing you can save on, because REI carries all kinds of outdoor clothing, skis, boots, shoes, bicycles, backpacking equipment, tents, tennis rackets, sleeping bags, long underwear, freeze-dried food, and everything else that has to do with sports and recreation.

Early Winters

RETAIL OUTLET
300 QUEEN ANNE AVENUE N.
284-4979
HOURS: MONDAY-SATURDAY 10:00-6:00

MAIL ORDER
110 PREFONTAINE PLACE S.
SEATTLE, WASHINGTON 98104
622-5203

CALL FOR FREE FULL-COLOR CATALOG.

Early Winters people are very proud of their store. They place an emphasis on unique selection, personalized customer service and on providing a congenial atmosphere. Their style might best be described as "organic" capitalism. Located on Queen Anne Hill in a deceptively small space, they have the world's largest selection of waterproof "breathable" Gore-Tex tents and rainwear, and carry many other high-quality outdoor items as well. Much of their merchandise is available nowhere else. Early Winters established its national reputation as a designer and maker of first-rate outdoor gear with the Omnipotent, a highly acclaimed little wonder that's been to the top of the most challenging mountains in the world. As a matter of fact, much of the merchandise in the store is of their own design, and made right here in Seattle. All the goods carry a lifetime warranty as well as their terrific "no-ifs-ands-or-buts" guarantee . . . which says that if you're not fully satisfied with any product after 30 days, bring it back for a full, friendly refund or exchange. Just like that. Now that's the way to run a business!

Gregg's Greenlake Cycle

**7007 WOODLAWN
AVENUE N.E.
(Ravenna Boulevard
at Greenlake Way)
523-1822
523-1819 service
department
HOURS:
MONDAY-FRIDAY
9:30-9:00
SATURDAY &
SUNDAY 9:30-6:00**

If it has wheels, chances are you can roll out of Gregg's Greenlake Cycle on it. This huge store takes up an entire block, accommodating the Northwest's largest selection of bicycles, tricylces, mopeds, and roller skates for sale or rent. It also has the distinction of being the largest Peugeot dealership in the country. For 47 years and 3 generations, the Gregg family has been offering a wide variety of quality products by Raleigh, Peugeot, Motobecane, Univega, Fuji and more. Whether you're a beginner or a racer, whether you're making a serious purchase or just renting for a day's adventure, you'll find the equipment and accessories ready to go. Gregg's is located at the hub of cycle activity in Seattle, just across from Greenlake and a couple of minutes from the Burke Gilman Trail . . . . so you can literally walk in and roll out. Visa. Master Charge. TransAction. Financing available.

 Fiorini Sports

4720 UNIVERSITY VILLAGE PLAZA
523-9610
HOURS: MONDAY-FRIDAY 9:30-9:00
SATURDAY 9:30-6:00
SUNDAY 11:00-5:00
CLOSED SUNDAYS APRIL 1-AUGUST 31

Buzz Fiorini is a real fixture in the Seattle sports scene, and has been from the time he started his famous ski school in 1947. Since then, Fiorini Sports has become an important tradition for active outdoor people in town. Originally started as a service to the ski school, the shop quickly expanded into other arenas, like tennis, backpacking, swimming and running. Fiorini Sports carries the best lines in athletic equipment . . . K2, Olin, Rossignol, Tyrolia, Hanson, Nordica, Roffe, Demetre, Davis, Adidas, Sierra Designs, North Face and many others. The service department is especially well-equipped, providing complete ski and binding mounting and maintenance, custom boot-fitting and repair, custom racquet stringing and other services. The staff are enthusiastic and helpful. In fact, Fiorini Sports regards their individual areas of expertise as a very integral part of the business . . . and it shows!
Visa. Master Charge. TransAction.

The Northface

4560 UNIVERSITY WAY N.E.
633-4431
HOURS: MONDAY-WEDNESDAY,
SATURDAY 10:00-6:00
THURSDAY, FRIDAY 10:00-9:00
SUNDAY 12:00-4:00

The Northface is where the U.S. Forest Service shops. It's known nationwide for developing new and better products for backpacking and mountaineering. The first geodesic tents were developed by Northface, along with some of the newest pack designs in outdoor gear technology.

The firm also supplied the tents used by the Bicentennial Mt. Everest expedition. Northface is mainly a manufacturing firm, but its Seattle shop was opened four years ago to offer Seattleites an alternative to run-of-the-mill gear. The shop sells the kind of equipment professionals prefer: Woolrich woolens, Robbins clothing and climbing equipment, Yak Paks, and Galibier Boots. You'll find quality equipment for ski touring here, too. As you'd expect, the Northface staff is knowledgeable and very familiar with their products. They frequently work with guide services and try to function as an information center. So, if you need information on where to go or what to do, as well as the gear that goes with it, the Northface is a fine place to discover.
Visa. Master Charge. American Express.

Zig Zag River Runners

TERMINAL SALES BUILDING, ROOM 403
1932 1ST AVENUE
382-0900
HOURS: MONDAY-FRIDAY 9:00-5:00
ADDITIONAL RESERVATIONS:
R.E.I. TRAVEL 322-7800
DOUG FOX TRAVEL 628-6151

When experienced white water boatman Jim Fiedler started Zig Zag River Runners 3 years ago, he chose the spirit of the great Sioux warrior Crazy Horse as his mythical leader. The business was named for the lightning flashes that protected the chief. Jim is wise about the ways of nature, and the proof is his perfect record with the hundreds of people he has taken rafting down rivers in Washington and throughout the world. Daily river rafting trips are offered nearly year-round, providing exciting whitewater thrills or beautiful float trips through eagle country. The whitewater trips are available daily, April through October. During early spring whitewater, Zig Zag takes you down the Wenatchee River, from pine forest to open sagebrush country, through a series of exciting, turbulent rapids. During summer months, they challenge the Suiattle River in the north Cascades, a dynamic little glacier-fed river with 10 miles of thrilling, non-stop whitewater action. If your taste runs to more placid paths, the Eagles float trip offered on weekends from December through February, takes you down the Skagit River, through the largest bald eagle wintering grounds outside Alaska. These magnificent birds perch in cottonwoods undisturbed as you glide by. Zig Zag offers other adventures as well, taking travelers on 10-day river expeditions through Alaska, 16 days on exotic rivers in South America and wildlife tours on eight of Washington's most scenic rivers. Reservations must be made 4 to 6 weeks in advance: day trips are $32 to $40 per person; prices vary for longer excursions.

The Runner's Place

321 BROADWAY AVENUE E.
324-6537
HOURS: MONDAY-FRIDAY 10:00-6:00
SATURDAY 10:00-6:00
SUNDAY 12:00-5:00

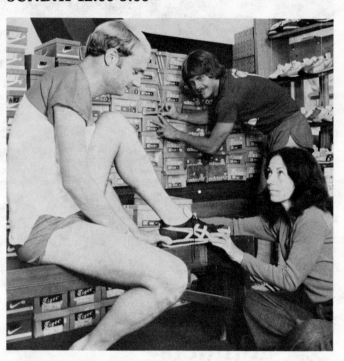

This terrific-looking store on Broadway caters to a runner's every need, carrying shoes, clothing, socks, hats, books, stop watches, and comforting aids for blisters and such. Sizes for men, women and children are available, along with practical, all-weather running gear that's perfect for our unpredictable weather. You'll find all the best brands: clothing lines like Bill Rodgers, Adidas, Sportco, GUTS, Dolphin, Winning Ways, and, especially designed with women runners in mind, Moving Comfort. The running and soccer shoe selection includes New Balance, Etonic, Nike, Adidas, Brooks, Tiger and Puma. The choice of shoes calls for expert attention to fit and individual need, a service that the Runner's Place takes seriously. Owners Judith Rockom and Gary Olsen spend a lot of time discussing fit and injury problems with customers, educating them about running and the importance of the right equipment. Between them, these two have 20 years running experience, so they know their way around the track.

The Swallow's Nest

3320 MERIDIAN AVENUE N.
633-0408
HOURS: MONDAY-TUESDAY 10:00-6:00
WEDNESDAY-FRIDAY 10:00-8:00
SATURDAY 10:00-5:00

The Swallow's Nest may not be the biggest mountaineering and ski-touring shop in Seattle, but their service, knowledge and dedication to the sport add up to make it outstanding. The store is named for the traditional first-night bivouac site on the north face of the Eiger in Switzerland, so when these folks talk about mountain climbing, they mean the real thing. They have a moderate-sized selection of the very best brands and designs of equipment, including Chouinard climbing hardware, Patagonia and Robbins clothing, and their own hand-crafted Swallow rain gear and packs, featuring Gore-Tex and coated nylon. Cross-country enthusiasts will find everything they need: boots, bindings, poles and skis from Epoke, Fisher, Kneissl, Atomic and Trak. If you want the finest equipment or just good, straight advice, The Swallow's Nest is the place to go.

Sturtevant's Sports

622 BELLEVUE WAY N.E.
BELLEVUE
454-6465

2016 SOUTH 320TH
BUILDING TWO
FEDERAL WAY
941-6560

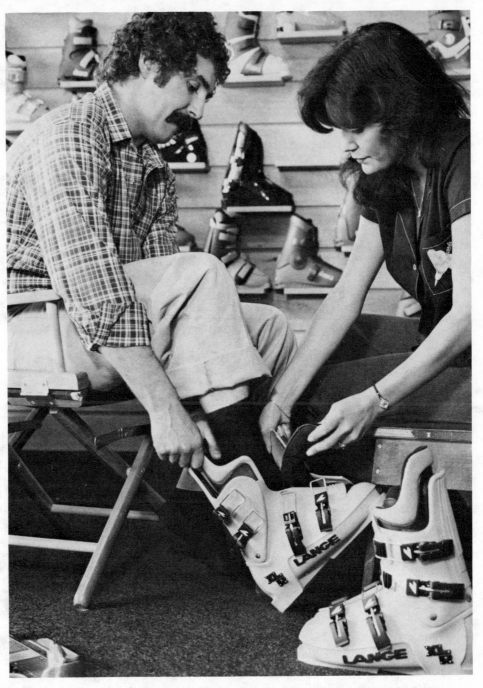

HOURS: MONDAY-FRIDAY 9:30-9:00
SATURDAY 9:30-6:00
SUNDAY 12-5:00

When skiing season rolls around, the first thing to do is think snow. The second thing is to think Sturtevant's Sports. That thought comes naturally to most skiing enthusiasts in Seattle since this store has been a leading ski outlet here for 16 years. They've got it all and in brand names skiers have come to trust over the years: skis from K2, Olin, Head, Rossignol, Pre and Atomic; boots by Hanson, Nordica, Dynafit, Scott and Lange; and the best clothing lines the world over . . . Anba, Bogner, Demetre, Head, JanSport, The Line, Roffe and Serac. Sturtevant's is a place where customer service is truly important. Salespeople are all experienced skiers who know the products and special needs of skiers in the area. They are very good at advising beginners and won't razzle-dazzle you with fancy sales pitches or sell you more ski than you really need. Of course, expert skiers will tell you that those are the reasons they've been sending people to Sturtevant's Sports for years. Visa. Master Charge. TransAction.

Warshal's Sporting Goods

**1000 - 1ST AVENUE
LOCATED HALFWAY
BETWEEN PIKE PLACE
MARKET AND PIONEER
SQUARE
624-7300
HOURS: MONDAY-
SATURDAY 9:00-5:30
FRIDAY UNTIL 9:00**

Warshal's Sporting Goods Company is a part of Seattle's history. It began in 1913 as a pawn shop in fact, but has evolved over the years into one of the city's foremost sporting goods outlets. The range is very comprehensive . . . hunting and fishing equipment, camping and boating supplies, all kinds of athletic gear and outdoor and sports clothing. The gun department offers all sizes, types and brands, including Smith & Wesson, Colt, Ranger, Winchester, Remington and more. The full-service gun repair shop employs three full time gunsmiths whose reputation for quality work is widely known. For fishermen, Warshal's has a superb, all-season selection of tackle and equipment that is kept fully-stocked year round. Informational clinics and demonstrations are held to introduce the latest products. The athletics department carries running clothes and a shoe selection boasting over 160 different models by all the well-known leading brands. There is also specialized footwear for hunters, fishermen and hiking enthusiasts. Prices are very reasonable in a range of affordable goods to specialized merchandise noted for quality. Generations of sportspeople have shopped at Warshal's because they know they can depend on consistent service, selection and competitive prices. All major bank cards. House Accounts. Lay-away plans.

Books

Photo: Historical Society of Seattle & King County

*Here was a city with water in its eyes and water in its belly. You couldn't have much more water
and still remain afloat.*

Alan Furst, ''Heart of the Reigning Queen''

A.R.C.

91 YESLER WAY
623-6798
HOURS: MONDAY-
SATURDAY 11:00-6:00
SUNDAY 12:00-5:00

A.R.C. or Arts Resource Center is just what you'd hope it would be from its name . . . the place where you'll find that wonderful art publication you saw in New York but haven't seen anywhere since. If you're not looking for anything specific, A.R.C. will open up the heart and ozone of the contemporary art world for you. Owner Diane Shepardson designed the store to promote visual awareness and serve as a resource for both artists and art lovers. Then she embellished it with extras . . . so you'll not only find beautiful art books, exhibition posters, photographic magazines, and other art publications, but a whole metropolis of postcards, an impressive collection of rubber stamps, and avant-garde European fashion magazines as well. Art Resource Center also hosts national invitational art shows. The recent ''Dog Show'' and ''Fish Show'' were both favorably reviewed.
Visa. Master Charge.

Arbur Books

4505 UNIVERSITY WAY N.E.
632-4204
HOURS: MONDAY-
FRIDAY 10:00-9:00
SATURDAY 10:00-6:00
SUNDAY 12-5:00
except summer.

Arbur Books is simply a great little bookstore in the University District, a neighborhood that used to be dominated by great big bookstores. And it's thriving, because owners Cynthia Burdell and Sally Argo have created the kind of shop that book people find totally comfortable. The place is laid out in a most logical fashion, from the really good collection of periodicals just inside the door to a well-chosen array of calendars and appointment books in the back. In between, there are shelves and tables of books; all kinds of books. They are particularly strong in literature, and have many paperbacks you're not likely to find in larger stores. Arbur also carries the best in science fiction and a good non-fiction sampling in both paperback and hardbound titles. The people who work there are friendly and knowledgeable, and if on the odd chance that one of them can't point you to the right shelf, a regular customer probably can.
Visa. Master Charge.

Miller & Mungo

Booksellers

81 S. WASHINGTON STREET
623-5563
HOURS: MONDAY-FRIDAY 10:00-6:00
SATURDAY 12-6:00

Miller & Mungo is not a general, and surely not a typical, bookstore. It caters to a particular book-buying audience, an audience bound with graphic designers and architects, calligraphers and typographers, bookbinders and papermakers. The store stocks a complete selection of Dover Publications, of the Global Architecture series from Tokyo, of the Graphis annuals. This is a carefully planned and operated bookstore; the salespeople know what books they have, where to find others. The Dover series provides a massive assortment of pictorial archive books, of both paperback and hardcover art books. Also, in the Dover group, reprinted mystery writers like Van Gulik and Le Fanu, reprinted music scores, a vast array of classic children's coloring books. All of these are in current stock. When available, the store has superb selections of Japanese rice paper, marbled papers and rag stationery.
Visa. Master Charge.

 # City News

10116 N.E. 8TH
BELLEVUE
455-9683
HOURS: MONDAY-SATURDAY 9:30-7:00
SUNDAY 12:00-5:00

City News is the best place in Bellevue to practice the fine art of browsing. This terrific magazine store stocks 900 foreign and domestic magazines, newspapers from all over the country, and a couple of thousand quality paperbacks. The periodicals cover nearly every subject: literature, aviation, sports, fashion, home decorating, business, photography, radio, sciences, automobiles, art and even muscle-building. The children's magazine selection is especially good. Newspapers come from all the major cities in the country as well as all over Washington state. Owner Harriet Bryant also keeps a comprehensive, up-to-date bulletin board that tells what's happening all over the city.
Master Charge. BankAmericard. TransAction.

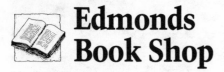 # Edmonds Book Shop

111 - 5TH AVENUE S.
EDMONDS, WASHINGTON
775-2789
HOURS: MONDAY-FRIDAY 10:00-6:00
SATURDAY 10:00-5:00

Jim and Betty Morrow moved here from Chicago, looking to settle in some of this famous scenery and open a bookstore. They found just the thing in the Edmonds Book Shop. They've been busy ever since *not* missing Eastern winters, and improving the book shop's service to the Edmonds community. They try to gear their selection to books that are of most current interest to people, and have come up with a good mixture of home improvement and decorating books, carefully chosen cookbooks, psychology titles, art books, a lovely children's section and of course, lots of quality fiction. Betty spent 15 years working in a small bookstore before moving west, so she's put lots of effort into making the Edmonds Book Shop distinctive and unique. To that end, there is a special focus on nautical titles and books about the Northwest and the islands . . . themes most relevant to the shop's beautiful west coast setting.
Visa. Master Charge.

The Elliott Bay Book Company

**1ST AVENUE S.
AT MAIN STREET IN PIONEER SQUARE
624-6600
HOURS: MONDAY-SATURDAY
10:30 AM-11:00 PM
SUNDAY 12 NOON-6:00 PM**

The Elliott Bay Book Company is probably the most attractive all-around bookstore in Seattle. It's certainly one of the most spacious, with balconies and split levels, and plenty of room to move around among the red cedar shelves and tables that hold their stock of over 40,000 titles. The emphasis is on literary volumes, including general fiction, science fiction, fantasy, mystery, poetry, drama and collected essays and criticism, but you can expect to locate a title or two on just about every imaginable other subject. There's a large children's section set apart from the rest of the store, a bargain book alcove which offers low prices on books that have for whatever reason gone ignored by the book industry . . . and plenty of stationery, postcards, posters, and they have also recently added prints from the New York Graphic Society. Elliott Bay Books has always had a special atmosphere, but now there's something new . . . a downstairs cafe, featuring espresso coffee and cafeteria service where, presumably, no-one minds if you read at the table.
Visa. Master Charge.

Dorothy B. Hughes Books

2322 6TH AVENUE
622-7866
HOURS: MONDAY-SATURDAY 9:30-5:00

Nationally known for its fine collection of books on metaphysics and astrology, the Dorothy B. Hughes bookstore started almost by accident. A devout astrologer for many years, Dorothy purchased three carloads of books from a store that went out of business. Since she had no place to put them all, she opened her bookstore, added extensively to the collection and soon had a very successful business. Dorothy had been teaching astrology classes even before she opened her shop and they are still offered, along with weekly lectures on the subject. Featuring the Northwest's best array of books on astrology, hypnotism, extrasensory perception, the I Ching, yoga and other disciplines, she also carries posters, tarot cards, and all the accessories you need for charting horoscopes. And, being a true Gemini, Dorothy is usually willing to take time to chat with customers and devotees of the field.

Quest Bookshop of Seattle

717 BROADWAY AVENUE E.
SEATTLE, WASHINGTON 98102
323-4281
HOURS: MONDAY-SATURDAY 12:00-6:00

The Quest Book Shop of Seattle is one of 6 similar bookshops in the United States owned and sponsored by the Theosophical Society. This facility functions as a metaphysical bookstore and information center, providing news about meetings and events in the Seattle area. Other subjects of interest at the shop are astrology, natural healing, herbology, psychology, science, religion, and energy. Authors and artists on the Quest shelves include David Spangler, Manley Palmer Hall, Christopher Hills, Dora van Gelder, Steven Halpern, Georgia Kelly, Allan Watts, C. G. Jung, Annie Besant and many others. The Quest Book Shop also has a large collection of cassettes and albums, featuring music and readings by noted authors. The price range is broad, from pamphlets for 25 cents to Manley Palmer Hall's magnificent book, The Secret Teachings of All Ages, for $95. The subscription library has a one-time deposit fee of $7.50. The library is restful, inviting and open most weekdays.

Cinema Books

701 BROADWAY AVENUE E.
323-5150
HOURS: MONDAY-SATURDAY 10:00-7:00
SUNDAY 12-7:00

It would suffice just to be the largest film book-store in the Northwest, but Cinema Books on Capitol Hill is also one of the best-looking bookstores as well. Cornered behind charming leaded windows in the historic Loveless Building, the shop is decked out with old movie posters, the latest film calendars and lots of intriguing show business related publications and such. There are film biographies, technical manuals, periodicals, books on criticism, scripts, picture books, history books, posters, stills, movie star cards, reference and trivia. You can literally name it; if it has anything to do with celluloid fantasies, Cinema Books either has it or can order it. Speaking of trivia: owner Stephanie Ogle may be Seattle's final authority when it comes to what Michael Rennie really said to the alien in *The Day the Earth Stood Still*. Go ahead, ask her anything. If you've hit one of the rare ones she doesn't know, the answer is only one shelf away at Cinema Books.

B. Bailey Books

RAINIER SQUARE
1301 - 5TH AVENUE
624-1328
HOURS: MONDAY-SATURDAY 9:30-5:30

It's hard to imagine a more pleasant place to shop for books than B. Bailey in the new Rainier Square. It has clearly been designed with book lovers in mind. Multi-leveled floors and shelves give a spacious feeling and encourage leisurely browsing. You also never know when you might be treated to an impromptu classical concert from the grand piano in the lobby outside the door. Owner Barbara Bailey puts time and care into her selection of books and is particularly proud of the well-stocked travel and business sections. Special orders are very welcome, so if you don't find what you need, feel free to ask. Visa. Master Charge.

Wide World Bookshop

401 N.E. 45TH STREET
634-3453
HOURS: MONDAY-SATURDAY 10:30-5:30

When you're debating whether to do the safari to Senegal or the jaunt to Jamaica; if you can't decide between getting away from it all or going where it's all happening, the first stop on your journey should be the Wide World Bookshop. Owned by inveterate travellers, the shop was launched to fill a need in Seattle: a complete selection of road maps, travel books, guides, language tapes, maps, globes, and everything else that has to do with travel. Even people who know exactly where they're going should stop at Wide World first to be prepared with details about their destination. If you have no idea where you want to go, but just feel restless, Garth and Royce Wilson can help you narrow it down. These two have travelled to some of the more unusual places in the world and love to trade stories and discuss trips with their customers. Their interest, expertise and outstanding selection combine to make Wide World Bookshop as essential to travel as passports and tickets.
Visa. Master Charge. TransAction.

Bluewater Books

SUITE 109, MARINERS SQUARE
1900 N. NORTHLAKE WAY
63BOOKS
HOURS:
MONDAY-SATURDAY 10:00-6:00

The best bookstores are owned by people who are in the business for the love of it. Bluewater Books is such a store. Owners Marcy and Mike McCarthy discovered an especially intriguing marine bookstore on a sailing trip to Australia and decided Seattle could use one too. They're as keen on sailing as they are on books about the sport; indeed all things nautical. It's an inventory designed for purpose or pleasure . . . novels, technical manuals, histories, children's books, calendars, note cards, art prints, log books. You can't find a more complete selection of marine titles in the city, and what they don't have they will gladly order. Other nautically relevant items are available at Bluewater Books too, like marine fixtures for home or boat, brass oil lamps; even jewelry and scrimshaw. It's a pleasure to visit a shop run by people whose business grew out of such an avid personal interest. Visa. Master Charge.

Crafts

Photo: Historical Society of Seattle & King County

Sitting there, listening to Charles Mingus on the stereo, I suddenly envisioned a shop of the same size in America, which would play Japanese koto music on its stereo. The right place for such a personal, quiet business would be Seattle. . . . There, I realized, I could have a business which enabled me to survive on very little money in a kind and easygoing environment.

Ray Mungo, "Return to Sender"

 # Ginny Conrow and Loretta Werner

Porcelain and Glass

1911 E. ALOHA STREET
324-0734
HOURS: MONDAY-SATURDAY 11:00-6:00

Ginny Conrow and Loretta Werner share a storefront studio at 19th and Aloha on Capitol Hill. These two talented artists work in different media but have a common dedication to their craft. Ginny Conrow is a potter, working exclusively in porcelain to create a variety of decorative and useful items . . . from cups, plates, French butter dishes and bowls to platters, vases, tea pots, lamps, tiles and even clocks. She applies her distinctive airbrushed and handpainted designs to each piece. Loretta Werner works in stained glass, using the copper foil method developed by the Louis Tiffany Company for three-dimensional pieces, and the leading technique for windows. She uses only the finest hand-selected imported and domestic glass to create boxes, candle-holders, planters, mirrors, lamps and windows. The delicate designs which she hand-paints and kiln-fires onto the glass give her work that special touch. Ginny and Loretta accept commissions for specific pieces and also offer gift certificates. The creations of both women are sold and displayed at leading galleries in New York, Boston, Los Angeles and Seattle, but people are welcome to stop by the studio to view their works-in-progress and purchase finished pieces.
Visa. Master Charge.

Collector's Quilts & Fabrics

301 E. PINE STREET
622-7217
HOURS: MONDAY-SATURDAY 10:30-5:30

Quiltmaking is a traditional American art, and Collector's Quilts & Fabrics is a store that nourishes that tradition in Seattle. They sell many new handmade quilts from all over the country, including those made by the Ohio Amish women, whose reputation and skill in the field are unmatched. Delicate antique quilts for the collector are also available, as well as reference books on the history of the art. Aspiring quiltmakers will find patterns, classes, demonstrations and the largest selection of 100% cotton print and plain fabric in the city. When you visit, be sure to get on their newsletter mailing list. Owner Sharon Yenter publishes an issue three times a year to keep her clientele informed of classes and a variety of special events. Visa. Master Charge.

Rob Landeros
Engravings in Ivory

(206) 367-3455
Please call for an appointment

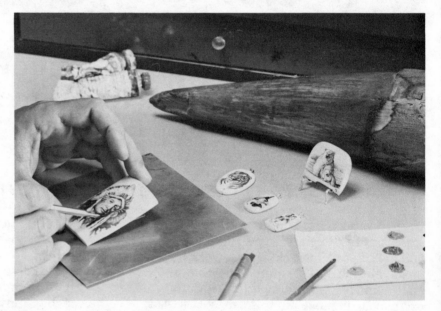

Scrimshaw is the American seafaring folk art of engraving in ivory or bone, and Rob Landeros is one of the country's finest scrimshaw artists. He uses only fossil ivory from prehistoric mastadon tusks, not only for its special richness and lustre of color and grain, but because he is opposed to killing living species for their ivory. Traditional scrimshaw is done with lampblack but Rob modifies the procedure to provide subtle shades of color as well. His is a small, exclusive and informal operation, specializing in custom designs and commissioned work. There are ready-made designs too . . . pendants, bracelets, tie tacks and bolo ties in gold and silver settings. Larger display pieces are also available, all featuring original designs by the artist. Visa. Master Charge.

Courtney Branch

Pottery & Housewares

109 S. MAIN STREET
622-2165
SEVEN DAYS A WEEK 10:00-5:30

Courtney Branch is a wonderful store. Well, actually, Courtney Branch is not just a store, it's a person. Or, rather, *he's* a person, who's known as one of the finest potters in the Northwest. Courtney's shop not only carries his beautiful and unusual hand-thrown stoneware and porcelain creations, but an eclectic selection of other carefully chosen objects as well. His own pieces include colorful casseroles, dinnerware, lamps, pots, vases and his remarkable sinks . . . an item you can't find in just any old pottery store. The rest of the shop is filled with big and small treasures from all over the world: exquisite batik fabrics from Indonesia and Malaysia, baskets from everywhere, cards and candles and soaps and kitchenware, rubber stamps and some of the most entertaining toys you've ever seen. Every visit seems to yield a new discovery. His pottery alone would be enough to sustain the interest, but Courtney Branch has successfully taken off in a dozen other directions as well . . . there's truly something for everyone.

Visa. Master Charge. TransAction.

 # Stewart & Stewart Pottery

1510 5TH AVENUE
622-7554
HOURS: MONDAY-SATURDAY 1:00-5:00
OPEN LATER BY SPECIAL ARRANGEMENT

Stewart & Stewart is so named because David and Leanne Stewart are a team . . . he makes pottery and she sells it. And they wouldn't have things any other way. One of the nicest things about this shop is that it's located right downtown, where small, family-owned handmade pottery shops do not exactly abound. The pottery is handmade in Seattle, except for a few pieces by Wally Schwab in Portland, and is very reasonably priced. David Stewart creates pots, casseroles and platters that can be used in the dishwasher, refrigerator, microwave, and (with caution) in a conventional oven. Other pieces, in both stoneware and porcelain include electric lamps, sinks, oil lamps, candle holders, coffee and tea pots, mugs, tumblers, bowls, pitchers, platters and honeypots. The electric lamps and sinks can be special-ordered for a particular glaze, design and size if you prefer. The pieces at Stewart & Stewart are free of lead or other harmful materials and come with complete instructions for proper care.
Visa. Master Charge.

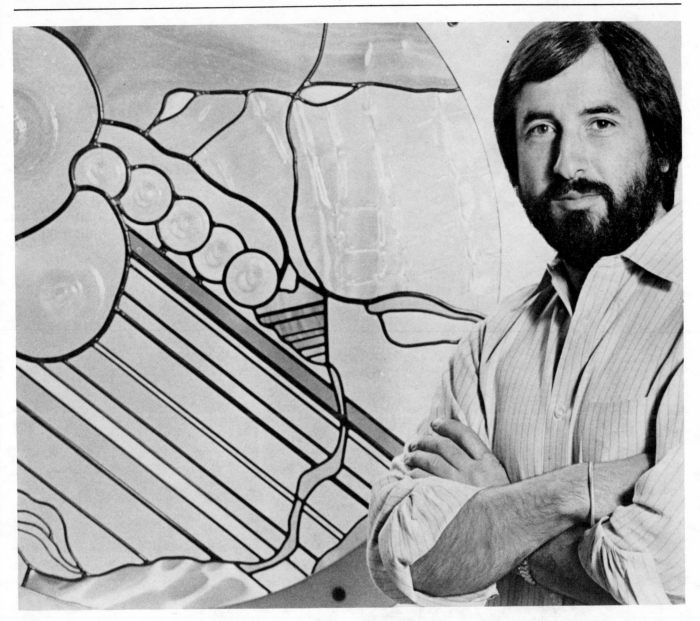

Glassworks

12718 NORTHRUP
BELLEVUE
455-4334
HOURS: MONDAY-FRIDAY 8:30-5:00

In a city known for its many leaded and stained glass studios, Glassworks is certainly one of the very best. Owner Steve Shahbaghlian and his staff of eight talented craftspeople have achieved national recognition for the quality, beauty and originality of their work. Some of this work has won awards and the shop has been featured in magazines. Steve himself has had four one-man shows and has had work shown in over three dozen galleries.

Glassworks is an active member of the Stained Glass Association, and they travel all over the U.S. to fulfill commissioned projects. Western International Hotels, Horatio's Restaurants, The Black Angus, and Clinkerdagger, Bickerstaff & Pett's Public House have all turned to Glassworks for the creation of pieces that highlight the design of these buildings . . .as only original works of art can. But their happiest clients are perhaps the many Seattle homeowners to whom even the greyest days look beautiful through the windows, skylights and custom-designed stained glass panels. Glassworks lends its expertise at every step, from design and execution through to installation. Ancillary services include abrasive glass etching, logos in glass, and names or designs applied to glass panels. Service is always prompt and consistent. The results . . . spectacular.

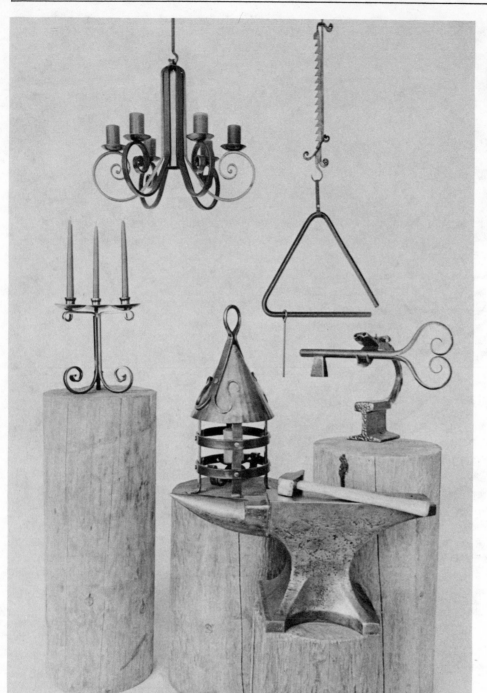

Enclume

**3241 EASTLAKE
AVENUE E.
325-4191
HOURS: MONDAY-
FRIDAY 8:30-5:00
SATURDAY 10:00-4:00**

Enclume is the French word for anvil and the last word in beautiful and functional hand-forged ironwork in Seattle. The business was started by craftsman Stuart Kendall, whose goal was to create objects of such quality that they would endure as heirlooms. He has succeeded. Enclume is a well-equipped shop, unique in its flexibility and capable of producing very small, delicate objects; or large pieces, aesthetically designed, yet strong and functional. Consistent, meticulous craftsmanship has become a tradition at Enclume, and is obviously the reason for the durability of the pieces produced here. These hand-made objects possess a depth of color and texture that you wouldn't normally associate with forged steel. The natural warm grey color of the carbon steel gives a glow that enhances any decor with an unmistakable look of quality. Included among the many beautiful items available through Enclume are chandeliers, lamps, candleholders, plant stands, clocks, fireplace accessories, and irons, gates and railings. Enclume also does some custom-design work, on a limited basis, for home and office construction projects. Visa. Master Charge.

The Glass Eye

1902 POST ALLEY
682-5929
523-2087 (Res)
HOURS: TUESDAY-SATURDAY 10:00-5:00
DESIGN STUDIO
BY APPOINTMENT ONLY

Hand-blown art glass is still in its infancy here in the U.S., but you can see this art form in full-blown glory at The Glass Eye. The Glass Eye is home to an exquisite collection created by six artists who enjoy a national reputation for their work. This studio/shop features every variation of art glass imaginable, both decorative and functional . . . vases, bowls, paperweights, wall panels, wine glasses, sculpture, lamp shades and windows. The colors are fabulous . . . rainbows and hues that shift and sparkle with the light. Pieces can be commissioned and the artists work closely with each client to achieve exactly the right effect. Artists at the Glass Eye also do quarterly shows at other galleries in town. They recently had a "fish show" at A.R.C., which also included artists from all over the United States. The work of less well-known artists is also displayed at The Glass Eye, whose members pride themselves in discovering untapped talent. If you've ever wondered about the elaborate process that goes into this craft, you might enquire about the classes offered.

Visa. Master Charge.

Woodcrafters

15040 N.E. 95TH ST.
REDMOND, WASHINGTON 98052
881-3636
HOURS: MONDAY-SATURDAY 9:00-6:00

Make furniture, mantels, countertops. Panel a wall or put down a floor. You'll find everything you need at Woodcrafters. This store carries the largest selection of hardwoods in the Pacific Northwest. They have maple, oak and ash from the forests of the Northwest, plus exotic hardwoods from Asia and the Phillipines. Woodcrafters, Inc. also has a good selection of veneers. There's an extensive line of carving tools and blocks, stains and finishes, and how-to-do-it books. Top brands featured include Henry Taylor woodworking tools, Minwax stains, Greenlee workbenches and imported Inca tools from Switzerland — the mercedes of power tools. Woodcrafters also makes their own hardwood paneling, available in unfinished oak or maple. All of the employees at Woodcrafters have been to the Bruce Company's "flooring school" and will be glad to give you pointers on installing your own hardwood floor. The store has a commercial division for professional cabinet and furniture makers, as well as the retail division for homeowners and craftspeople. If you have friends in Oregon, you might tell them there are Woodcrafter stores in Salem and Portland, too. Visa. Master Charge.

Occidental Art Glass

410 OCCIDENTAL SOUTH
SEATTLE
624-8200
TOLL FREE 1-800-426-9902
1-800-426-1830
HOURS: MONDAY-FRIDAY 9:00-5:30
SATURDAY 10:00-5:00

Occidental Art Glass looks more like a gallery than a retail store. Actually, it *is* more than a retail store — it is Seattle's premiere wholesale and retail glass supply house for stained glass art. This shop services both the collector and creator, carrying a full line of supplies as well as beautiful finished pieces. The stained glass comes from all over the world and

Occidental Art Glass carries over 1,000 different types of glass in every imaginable color. Glazier's tools are available here, and if you can't find what you need in stock, choose from the catalogue, a complete listing over 500 of the latest stained glass crafting tools. Owner David White and his experienced staff of craftsmen can create stunning stained glass windows, panels and Tiffany-type lamp shades for people who don't make their own. The complete self-service display room provides a beautiful setting for viewing the pieces. If what you want is in your mind's eye, the staff designers will create stained glass art to your specifications and will instruct you about care and maintenance of stained glass articles. This store is the one place in Seattle where bent, curved or slumped glass can be repaired. Restoration services are also offered for valuable heirlooms. Occidental Art Glass teaches beginning and advance classes in stained glass window and lamp-making techniques.
Visa. Master Charge.

Northwest Craft Center & Gallery

SEATTLE CENTER BETWEEN FOUNTAIN AND COLISEUM
624-7563
HOURS: 11:00-6:00 DAILY, CLOSED MONDAYS FROM LABOR DAY THRU MEMORIAL DAY

The Northwest Craft Center and Gallery has been around since 1963 and has a long reputation for its quality crafts. It also has the best view of any gallery in town, outside as well as in. One entire wall has windows facing the fountain in the Seattle Center, with lots of trees and lush grass. Inside is a handsome selection of handmade items for sale, created by as many as 200 artists from all over the Northwest. Quality is maintained by a careful jury process, and the designs and functions range from small whimsical pieces to large pottery. You'll also find two-dimensional art . . . paintings, watercolors, lithographs, serigraphs, jewelry, handmade books and notecards. The focus however is on the ceramic arts with an array of hand-thrown and slip-cast pieces both practical and decorative. Production of these pieces involve various firing techniques, such as salt glazing and raku. Featured artists include Tom Coleman, Bob Sperry, Ann Hirondelle, David Keys, and Harold Balazs. The Gallery conducts a regular schedule of individual and group shows highlighting the work of these and other artists. Visa. Master Charge.

Costume by Lynn di Nino

Gail Chase Gallery

22 103RD AVENUE N.E.
BELLEVUE
454-1250
HOURS: TUESDAY-SATURDAY 10:00-5:30
OPEN MOST MONDAYS

Gail Chase belongs to a vanishing breed . . . the romantic adventuress. The exotic islamic items in her gallery, scattered among the other pieces, give you something of a clue to her intriguing background, but it's best to hear it from her because she spins a good tale. Suffice to say that she has travelled the oases of the world, been held in a Turkish prison as a spy, entertained by camel caravans in Timbuktu and by Berber religious mystics in the Sahara. Her current adventure is the gallery, which houses the largest selection of ceramics and tapestries in the Northwest. This is the only crafts gallery in the Seattle area not limited to the work of local artists. About half the collection *is* local but the rest is juried by American Crafts Council members from all over the United States. Gail's selection is informed, since she was a practising and teaching ceramicist for 20 years. A suburban surprise, you'll find this exotic little oasis right in the Bellevue business district.
Visa. Master Charge.

 **Seattle
Pottery Supply**

**400 E. PINE STREET
SEATTLE 98122
(206) 324-4343
HOURS: MONDAY-FRIDAY 9:00-5:00
SATURDAY 10:00-2:00**

It would seem that if your are a potter, Seattle is the place to be. After all, the largest collection of pottery books in the country is right here, at Seattle Pottery Supply on Capitol Hill. This marvelous store caters to everyone from the novice potter to the experienced craftsman. As the largest pottery supplier in the Northwest, they manufacture "SPS" clay and glazes, carry Westwood clay, Shimpo wheels, Olympic kilns and accessories, Alpine equipment, Kemper tools and many other major names, including hard-to-find and unusual brands.

Owner Jim Lunz, not content to operate a mere supply store, has also added special services like custom mixes of clay, rental studio space for potters, classes at all levels of expertise, and even a gallery on the second floor where the artists' work is displayed. Customers may depend upon knowledgeable advice, because staff people at Seattle Pottery Supply are all involved themselves in the creation of pottery.
Visa. Master Charge.

 # Jewelry

Photo: Historical Society of Seattle & King County

The sun was squandering itself out over the Olympics, frosty and cold over on the western horizon.

Lorenzo Milam

Fox's Gem Shop

**1341 - 5TH AVENUE
RAINIER SQUARE
623-2528
HOURS: MONDAY-SATURDAY 9:30-5:00**

Fox's Gem Shop is Seattle's answer to Tiffany's in New York. First established in 1948 when Sidney and Berta Thal scraped together just enough capital to buy the existing business, Fox's has become a highly respected jeweler nationally and internationally. It bears all the style, dignity and dazzle of Tiffany's, with a measure of warmth that is uniquely Fox's. Their new store in Rainier Square is simply magnificent. An achievement the Thal's are deservedly proud of, the store has 5,000 square feet of beautifully appointed, warmly lit space with elegant Italian wall coverings and custom-made display cases. The gems and jewelry are, as you might expect, beautiful and always of the finest quality. Fox's has developed a collection to rival the best in the country. They have a genuine concern for their clients. In Sidney Thal's own words: "I'd put integrity first, having people believe in us and our merchandise." With that attitude uppermost, there is never an effort to "sell" customers at Fox's. In fact, the Thals have been known to discourage people from buying jewelry that seemed unsuited to them. It's this kind of enlightened business sense, along with dedication to their craft, that has given Fox's top status in the jewelry field.
Visa. Master Charge. American Express. Diners Club.

Scandia Jewelers

**814 SECOND AVENUE
(AT MARION)
682-RING
HOURS: MONDAY-FRIDAY 10:00-5:30
SATURDAY BY APPOINTMENT ONLY**

Those with an eye for contemporary designs will recognize the quality of the workmanship behind the creations at Scandia Jewelers. The talent of Paul Burns and Rick Davis has made Scandia a landmark for Seattle jewelry design. It's a spot largely removed from the city center's bustle, where clients know they'll be able to sit down in an unhurried atmosphere and personally discuss their own ideas with a master craftsman, who has the skill to render a completely satisfying interpretation. Scandia also offers a beautiful selection of Kusak Crystal and famous hand-blown art glass, jewelry and other fine gifts. It's a truly unique jewelry store.

Visa. Master Charge. American Express. Carte Blanche.

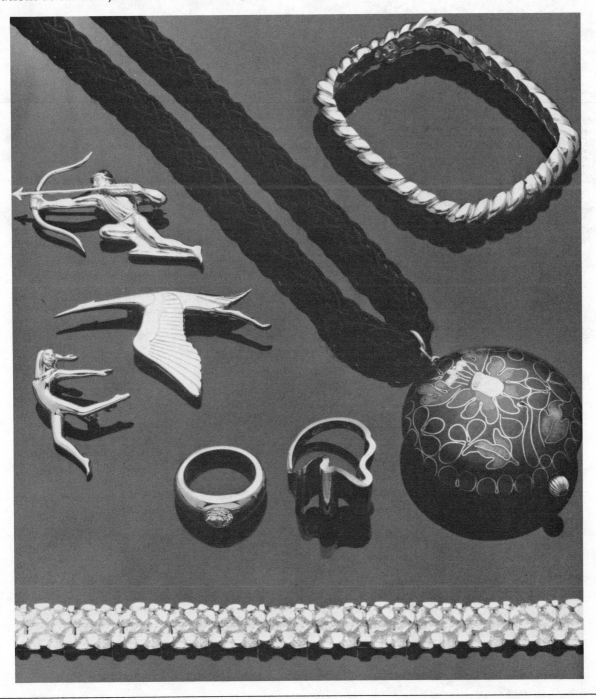

Robin's Jewelers

220 1ST AVENUE S.
GRAND CENTRAL ON THE PARK
PIONEER SQUARE
622-4337
HOURS: MONDAY-FRIDAY 10:00-5:30
SATURDAY 10:30-5:00

Robin's Jewelers is, like many of the best things, not terribly easy to find, but definitely worth looking for. Tucked away in the historic Grand Central Building, Robin's has a very original jewelry collection and it's beautifully displayed. Along with classic gold and diamond pieces, they have incorporated other dazzling gemstones . . . rubies, emeralds, topaz, tourmaline in any color of the rainbow, and lapis lazuli. Custom design service is the sign of the best jewelers and Robin's is no exception. They enjoy creating individual designs for people who want different, yet wearable jewelry. If you have a favorite design, they can suggest the best way to realize your creation in the most fashionable, elegant manner. Robin's also sells fine antique clocks for the collector or investor. Visa. Master Charge.

Philip Monroe, Jeweler

**Registered Jeweler,
Certified Gemologist,
American Gem Society**

**527 PINE STREET
624-1531
HOURS: MONDAY-SATURDAY 9:30-5:30**

Philip Monroe is regarded as one of the finest jewelry designers in the country, and consequently has many devoted clients. His shop in downtown Seattle, across from Frederick and Nelson, is not at all the usual jewelry store with rows and rows of look-alike rings and watches. It is a small, elegantly-appointed place with antique furnishings, polished wood and Chinese screens. Customers are encouraged to make themselves comfortable and take their time viewing the selection. There are rings, bracelets, necklaces and brooches as well as more unusual collectors items such as an exquisite Faberge duck, a sinuous leopard with glittering gemstone eyes and Mr. Monroe's own original design pieces. He creates unusual and unique jewelry to a client's specifications, after a discussion of the best settings and precious metals to combine with particular stones. He also transforms older, out-dated jewelry into beautiful new designs that reflect today's more casual attitudes about wearing fine jewelry. If you have an heirloom you would only trust in the hands of the very best, Philip Monroe, Jeweler, is an excellent choice.
Visa. Master Charge. American Express.

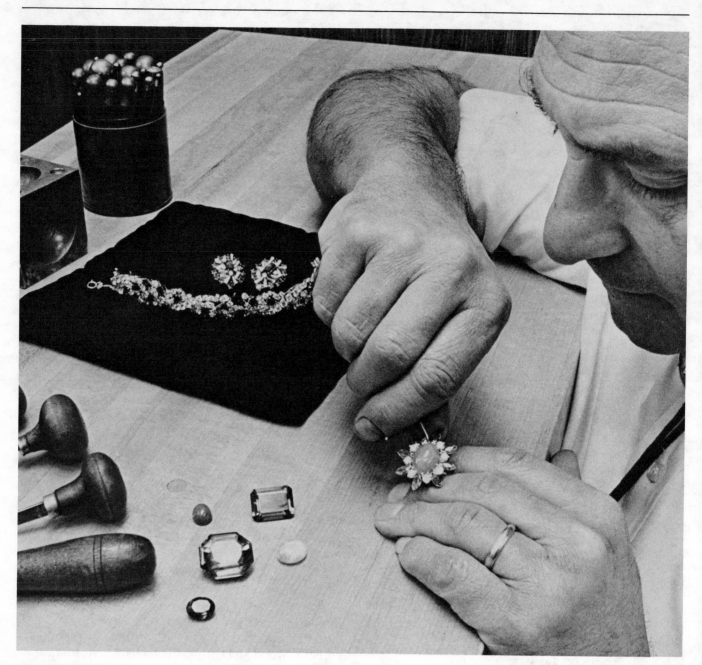

Azose & Son

2018 - 3RD AVENUE
622-5323
HOURS: MONDAY-THURSDAY 9:30-5:30
FRIDAY - BY APPOINTMENT ONLY

Upon entering the establishment of Azose & Son you quickly realize that you aren't in an ordinary jewelry store. Delightfully elegant and subtle creations of gold and precious stones meet the eye. Behind tinted partitions, master goldsmiths engage in the work of custom manufacturing one-of-a-kind pieces of jewelry. It is this special work that sets Azose & Son apart. Proprietor Sol Azose and his son Larry proudly display the latest pieces in their collection. They oversee every step of the design and production of each item to ensure that it meets their standards of excellence. The client can relax in the comfortable atmosphere to view the selection of fine gemstones and diamonds. You may also have your gems expertly appraised, or take advantage of the complete gemological laboratory for the cleaning and maintenance of your fine jewelry. Their jewelry is beautiful, but it's the personal attention and service that has made Azose & Son a Northwest institution for over 60 years.
Visa. Master Charge.

Art

Photo: Historical Society of Seattle & King County

The sunshine in Seattle seeps up from the ground through roots to stems and trunks of plants and trees and is radiated by a billion leaves, lending the clouds, rolling low, their green glow.

Spencer Holst

 # Seattle
Art Museum

**VOLUNTEER PARK
ON CAPITOL HILL
447-4710
HOURS: TUESDAY-SATURDAY 10:00-5:00
TUESDAY & THURSDAY EVENINGS
7:00-10:00
SUNDAY 12:00-5:00**

**MODERN ART PAVILLION
AT SEATTLE CENTER
2ND AVENUE & THOMAS STREET
447-4795
HOURS: TUESDAY-SUNDAY 11:00-6:00
THURSDAY UNTIL 8:00**

The Seattle Art Museum provides the public with one of the Northwest's most interesting and varied collections of visual arts. The permanent exhibitions are a source of pride. They include an extensive group of Asian arts, near east and classic objects, a Western art exhibit, tribal artifacts and a fine 19th Century/Pacific Northwest art collection. The shows and collections brought to Seattle and the Northwest by the Museum are elected for their importance, magnificence and diversity. The museum in Volunteer Park was built by the founder, Dr. Richard Fuller, and his mother. Upon its completion in 1933, the Fullers gave the building to the City of Seattle. The Modern Art Pavillion is located in the Seattle Center and was renovated after the World's Fair. The museum is raising money to build a new facility in the heart of the city, in order to exhibit more of its collection and augment its already considerable services to the public.

The Henry Art Gallery

ON THE UNIVERSITY OF WASHINGTON CAMPUS
543-2280

The Henry Art Gallery is an important cultural resource that serves the entire city. This beautiful gallery draws support from the University of Washington which houses it, as well as from the Henry Art Gallery Association. This backing enables the gallery to bring to Seattle major works and comprehensive collections from all over, featuring leading traditional and contemporary artists. Each show goes beyond simple exposition of the work itself to include a host of related printed materials, carefully compiled to offer explanation and reviews of the exhibited pieces. This approach is further reinforced through a series of lectures and educational programs about the work and its influences. Each year, the Henry Art Gallery presents the Fall Lecture Series, which offers a full complement of programs on selected subjects in the arts. The gallery regularly schedules shows throughout the year, each highlighting individual artists of different schools of painting, such as the recent 19th Century American Impressionism exhibit. The Henry Gallery Association is open to all and they welcome the support new members provide the gallery.

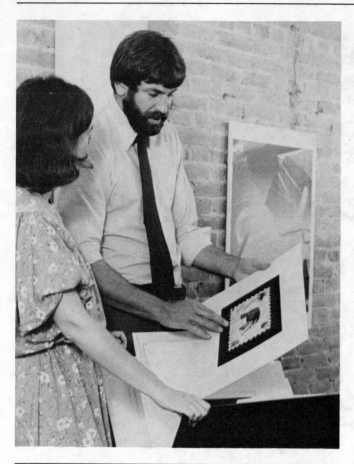

Davidson Galleries

702 - 1ST AVENUE
624-7684
HOURS: TUESDAY-SATURDAY
12 NOON-5:00 PM

The Davidson Gallery, at the north end of Pioneer Square, deals exclusively in fine prints. Fine prints are art reproductions taken from a surface prepared by the artist himself. The gallery is a small, well-designed and interesting space, with room for comfortable browsing. Prints are on the wall and stored in bins where they can be easily reviewed. The collection is extensive and includes original etchings, woodcuts, serigraphs and lithographs. There are engravings by Durer, Rembrandt, Blake and Goya, woodblock prints of Hiroshige and Hokusai. Northwest printmakers are well-represented too; Carl Chew, Art Hansen and D.G. Smith among them . . . as well as manuscript fragments and other interesting oddments.

 # Foster/White Gallery

311½ OCCIDENTAL AVENUE S.
622-2833
HOURS: MONDAY-SATURDAY 10:00-5:30
SUNDAY 12-5:00

Foster/White is Seattle's largest and certainly one of the most respected art dealers. Established in 1967, the gallery is located in a beautiful, high-ceilinged, spacious loft in Pioneer Square on Occidental Mall. Foster/White represents work by some of the most important Northwest sculptors and painters, including Mark Tobey, Morris Graves and Kenneth Callahan. Exhibitions change every three weeks, and include paintings, drawings and sculpture. The gallery is divided into four distinct spaces, so one is sure to encounter a full range of interesting possibilities at every show.

Linda Farris Gallery

322 - 2ND AVENUE S.
623-1110
HOURS: MONDAY-SATURDAY 11:30-5:00
SUNDAY 1:00-5:00
THURSDAY UNTIL 8:00

It's hard to imagine Pioneer Square without the Linda Farris Gallery. One of the earliest factors in the revitalization of this vibrant neighborhood, the gallery now approaches its 10th anniversary. In those ten years, much progress has taken place in Seattle's degree of enthusiasm for modern art. Anyone who feels part of this phenomenon will agree that Linda's contribution has been major. The gallery focuses on museum-quality shows of contemporary art by regional and national artists. She has hosted special exhibitions for people like Robert Rauschenberg and Louise Nevelson. Linda also represents 20 Seattle artists, including Gertrude Pacific (this Catalogue's cover artist) and Sherry Markovitz whose paintings are depicted above. Every kind of art is represented, including sculpture, prints, drawings and paintings. The gallery also offers educational programs and art consultation for both commercial and private clients on subjects such as framing and installation of collections.

Traver Gallery

2219 FOURTH AVENUE
622-4234
HOURS: TUESDAY-SUNDAY 12:00-5:00
THURSDAY EVENING 12:00-9:00

For many artists the hardest place to gain recognition and establish a name is at home, so they're forced to seek other markets. To curb the exodus of talented artists and friends, Anne and Bill Traver opened this gallery which presents primarily the work of regional artists. Traver Gallery is a showcase for Seattle's sculptors, painters, and photographers who have something to say and who present fresh ideas in a compelling manner. Anne and Bill are active in the local art community and feel strongly that artists who deserve recognition should not have to abandon the special inspiration of this area. Andrew Keating is one of these artists. His paintings are displayed here, along with sculptures by Lee Kelly, and abstract paintings by Paul Heald. Dick Busher, an abstract photographer, and D.G. Smith, who does large figurative paintings and prints, are also represented. Anne and Bill consult with corporations, institutions, and private collectors about assembling collections. Their gallery has become one of the best sources of information about indigenous artists and Seattle's best young talent.

Diane Gilson Gallery

119 - 1ST AVENUE S.
622-3980
HOURS: TUESDAY-SATURDAY 10:30-5:30

The Diane Gilson Gallery is a pleasure to visit in part because of the space itself. Located in the lower level of the Maynard Building in Pioneer Square, this quiet gallery has a beautiful old ceramic floor and large windows permitting a natural light that enhances the display of the art. A piece in the permanent collection of special note is the door from the original vault of the Dexter Horton Bank still embedded in the gallery's wall. Diane Gilson deals in fine painting, sculpture and prints, from the Northwest and all over the country. She is the exclusive agent for such local artists as Alden Mason and Margaret Tomkins, but also shows work by New York and Los Angeles artists like Alice Neel, Paul Jenkins, Patrick Humble, Robert Motherwell, Helen Frankenthaler and others. Diane's experience in the art world is considerable: she is known as an authoritative art consultant to both corporate and private collectors.

Richard Hines Gallery

2030 5TH AVENUE
682-5630
HOURS: TUESDAY-SATURDAY 11:00-6:00

At the Richard Hines Gallery, things are done on a grand scale. The space itself is large, open and uncluttered, with high ceilings and windows on two sides . . . the art shown here measures up to the demands of such a dramatic setting. Dealing exclusively in paintings, sculpture and drawings by established, internationally recognized American artists such as Rauschenberg, Warhol, Lichtenstein, de Kooning and others, this gallery brings a different flavor to the Seattle art scene. Over the past year, there have been world premier shows of new work by major artists from both coasts, like Robert Rauschenberg, Edward Ruscha and James Rosenquist. The gallery has also shown sculpture by such noted artists as Anthony Caro, Donald Judd, Dan Flavin, Bruce Nauman, Michael Heizer and Carl Andre. The recent Richard Serra show was the largest American exhibition of his drawings to date. Mr. Hines also provides appraisals and is available for consulting with both private and corporate clients interested in collecting and investing.

Penryn Gallery

1920 1ST AVENUE
623-0495
HOURS: TUESDAY-SATURDAY 11:00-5:00
AN BY APPOINTMENT THROUGH 932-9560

It happens to the best people . . . you're casually walking down 1st Avenue, just above the Pike Place Market, when something in the window at the Penryn Gallery puts a turn in your step and your nose to the window. Next thing, you're stepping into the Penryn. This small gallery packs more punch per square foot than places twice its size. The Gallery gained its popularity long before the revival of the market area. Owner Paul Penryn Carkeek has been showing some of Seattle's brightest and most innovative artists at this location for 10 years. The Penryn Gallery deals in paintings, sculpture, prints, photographs, glass, textiles and ceramics, all geared to avid collectors who are interested in unique visual art forms. Among the artists represented here are Joan Ross Bloedel, Michael Gesinger, Ilene Meyer, Joyce Moty, Joe Reno, Sally Roberts, Mark Strathy, Steve Walker, Charley Brown, Barbara Berger, and Isabel Sim-Hamilton.

 # The Silver Image Gallery

**92 S. WASHINGTON STREET,
PIONEER SQUARE
623-8116
HOURS: TUESDAY-SATURDAY 11:00-5:30**

The Silver Image Gallery belongs to the community of nationally known and respected photographic galleries. This gallery is the West Coast pioneer in exhibiting photo art, and one of the oldest in the country. The masters are shown here . . . Ansel Adams, Imogen Cunningham, Edward Curtis, Winn Bullock, and Brett Weston, plus the talented generation that has followed . . . Michael and Marsha Burns, Richard Misrach, Karen Truax, and Ralph Gibson, to name a few. Owner Dan Fear has an impressive knowledge of 20th Century photography and he is widely regarded as an expert on collecting. Private and corporate collectors from Seattle and many other cities consult this gallery about acquisitions, yet the place retains a friendly, approachable quality that novice collectors find encouraging. The gallery offers affordable works by undiscovered artists with striking talent. The selection of photographs on hand is very impressive and available for viewing by appointment. If you're looking for a particular book on photography or a photographic poster, the Silver Image will save you time, and probably tempt you to buy two because their selection of publications and posters of note is so extensive. For information about current shows, call the gallery during business hours.
Visa. Master Charge.

 # Equivalents

Equivalents is a gallery specializing in fine art photography and is located on the second floor of a turn-of-the-century Victorian on Capitol Hill. The gallery is equally committed to the exhibition of work by artists who enjoy international reputations as well as work by lesser-known photographers. Equivalents represents some of the finest contemporary photographers in the country, presenting a wide range of photographic techniques which include both silver and non-silver processes. In addition, the gallery has prints available by such artists as Barbara Morgan, André Kertész, Danny Lyon, Walker Evans, Marion Post Wolcott and Felice Beato. The gallery's print and slide inventory is available for viewing upon request. Equivalents carries a fine selection of photography books, posters, postcards, darkroom supplies and film as well.

Visa. Master Charge.

 Creation Gallery

10837 N.E. 2ND PLACE
BELLEVUE
454-8535
HOURS: TUESDAY-SATURDAY 10:00-5:00

Creation Gallery sells fine investment art from all over the world, by such masters as Miro, Rockwell, Boulanger, Dali, Tobey, Eidenberger and the Kasimir family. But their services don't stop there, because owners Shirley Tavis and Linda Challman are expert design consultants who attach the same importance to framing, hanging and display as they do to the art itself. Framing is of course especially important, and Creation Gallery provides museum-quality work in this area. They will help you select frames to enhance the piece and fit the surrounding decor. This thorough approach has much to do with Creation Gallery's reputation as the best complete art service in Bellevue.

Bellevue Art Museum and Museum School

**10310 N.E. 4TH STREET
BELLEVUE
MUSEUM: 454-3322
SCHOOL: 454-3323
MUSEUM: TUESDAY-
SUNDAY 12:00-5:00
DOCENT TOURS 2:00 PM DAILY
OFFICE: 9:00-5:00**

The Bellevue Art Museum officially opened its doors in September 1975, after more than 25 years of dreaming and planning by the Pacific Northwest Arts and Crafts Association. Since that time, a good number of important exhibitions have been presented to the Seattle and Bellevue public, including "Japanese Wood Block Prints from the Sakai Collection" and "Eye for Eye: Egyptian Images and Inscriptions." The changing exhibitions feature art of local, regional, and national importance and are free. In existence since September 1973, the Bellevue Art Museum School offers a wide variety of art classes for young people and adults on a credit or non-credit basis. For further information on current Museum exhibitions or a schedule of art classes, call the Museum.

The Erica Williams/Anne Johnson Gallery

**317 E. PINE STREET
623-7078
HOURS: WEDNESDAY-SATURDAY
11:00-5:00**

The Erica Williams/Anne Johnson Gallery is just up from Frederick and Nelson on East Pine. It's a gallery of distinction because of the strong interest these two women share in promoting and exposing the talents of Northwest artists, in company with artists of well-established national fame. When the gallery first opened, its specialty was European prints, including those of Mark Tobey. Now, printmaking is featured in exhibits, along with painting, sculpture, and photography. The extensive list of popular Northwest artists whose work is shown here includes David Allison, Doris Chase, Diane Katsiaficas, Maxine Nelson, Bill Ritchie, and Robert Sperry. With its high walls and delightful balcony, the Erica Williams/Anne Johnson Gallery is a perfect host for the original prints by Mark Tobey, Anthony Topies, and Henry Moore. The Gallery serves as a consultant for banks, and offices, and will visit the home of clients who want special advice on their collection. Art appraisals are also a part of the service.

 # Panaca

376 BELLEVUE SQUARE
BELLEVUE
454-0234
HOURS: MONDAY-SATURDAY 10:00-5:30

Panaca is probably Bellevue's best known gallery. Established in 1961 by the Pacific Northwest Arts and Crafts Association, it serves as a year-round showcase for the best of the Northwest's talented artisans. Fine pottery, glass, jewelry, fibre arts and wood pieces are featured along with two-dimensional works available for sale or rental. The gallery selects work from developing young craftsmen as well as established artists, placing an emphasis on quality and tradition. Under the direction of Georgie Kilrain, Panaca is still operated as an arm of the Association. All monies from sales go to benefit the Bellevue Art Museum and Bellevue Art Museum School.

The Legacy

71 MARION VIADUCT
624-6350

The Legacy has been a source of the best contemporary and historical Northwest Indian and Alaskan Eskimo art for over 40 years. The collection that has evolved during that time is probably the most discriminating and varied one in Seattle. Owner Mardonna Austin-McKillop has a long experience collecting and appreciating the native art of our region, and she encourages customers to become well acquainted with the field before deciding on a purchase. Research materials are on hand in the thorough selection of text and picture books on Northwest coast and Alaskan art and serve to provide both novices and experienced collectors with information about the pieces on display. The Legacy's collection includes older treasures like an 1890's carved model canoe, chilkat blankets, elegant and graceful baskets, totems and ancient household articles . . . all bearing the strong, sculptural forms that give Northwest Indian art a cultural appeal. The contemporary pieces are equally beautiful — silver jewelry, soap-stone sculpture, limited-edition prints, carved wood masks, boxes, and bowls by such leading Northwest artists as Pasco, Thompson, Davidson, Livingston and Hunt; as well as rare photo-gravures by Edward Curtis. The Legacy also arranges for commissioned carvings executed by skilled artists whose work shows a studied respect for the traditions of Northwest native art.

Market Graphics

1935 1ST AVENUE
682-7732
HOURS: MONDAY-SATURDAY 10:00-6:00

Established in 1978, Market Graphics has quickly become one of the most popular poster and framing shops in Seattle. There are over 900 posters available, from sources all over the world. Market Graphics emphasizes event-oriented pieces that were commissioned for specific occasions, like gallery shows, festivals and performances. Market Graphics features the work of several Seattle artists, as well as such notables as David Lance Goines, Patrick Nagel, Georgia O'Keefe, Delacroix and Steinberg. The framing service is one of the city's best. You can have pieces framed here or purchase prepared and pre-cut components for framing at home. Owners Ann McGaffin and Sharon Hamilton will visit your home or office to help choose the frames or artwork to complement your decor, but don't pass up the chance to visit this store, because it's a visual treat. It's places like Market Graphics that have done so much to popularize an appreciation of art.
Visa. Master Charge.

Artech

169 WESTERN AVENUE W.
284-8822
HOURS: MONDAY-FRIDAY 9:00-5:00
OR BY APPOINTMENT

Handling fine art is a fine art and in Seattle, Artech does it best. This company is a group of dedicated, hard-working professionals, all of whom have backgrounds in art or extensive museum experience. Their first and most essential service is packing, shipping, and storing of art. The facilities and materials used are strictly the finest, providing maximum protection. Secondly, Artech provides installation and design of art. The city's leading galleries call on Artech to arrange everything from the physical placement of pieces, to overall exhibit design. This service addresses spatial and lighting considerations to assure that the work is displayed to its best advantage. Finally, Artech offers general collection management, including maintainence, upkeep, cataloguing, and photographic documentation. They employ museum-standard registration and records management techniques. The Artech client list proves their worth: Seattle Art Museum, the Seattle Arts Commission, the City of Seattle, Sea-First Bank, Rainier Bank, and most of Seattle's major contemporary galleries and private collectors. Artech offers three areas of service the world of art couldn't do without.

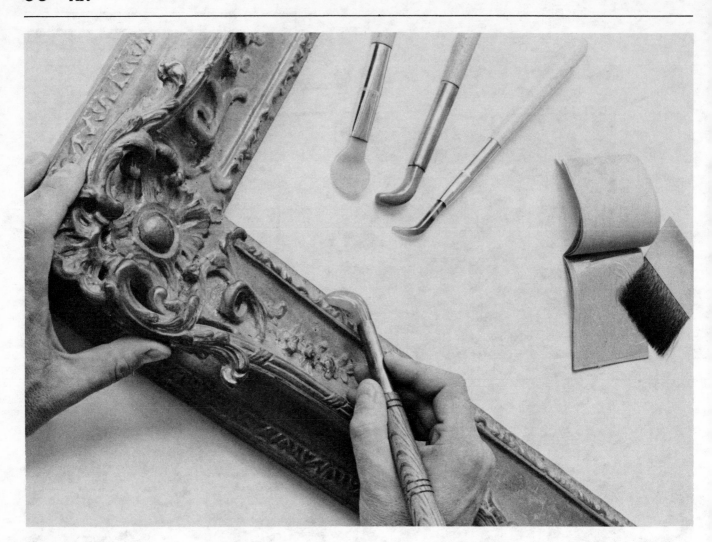

Denman Associates

2124 FIFTH AVENUE
SEATTLE
624-7024
HOURS: MONDAY-FRIDAY 9:00-5:00

Denman Associates excel in two important services to the art world. They provide a complete framing service from their downtown studio where art is framed with the expertise you'd expect from techniques personally learned in leading framing establishments in New York, London and Florence. A long involvement of over 30 years of buying art for themselves and others in major art centers in this country, Europe and the Orient, has provided a rich background for Jean and John Denman in the art consultation field, a service sought by collectors in Seattle and beyond. A tradition of museum quality in framing and selecting art forms the foundation for both areas of work. When they make replica carvings for period frames, the designs used are based on the best originals in the Prado, Uffizi, the Louvre and other great museums. Modern frames also are used in a wide range of materials, including waxed woods, genuine 23k gold leafing, welded aluminum, plexiglas and metal sectionals. The popular Plas-Wraps are also available for posters. The work of Denman Associates is first rate, and their command of knowledge about the current art market is employed in the consultation service.
Visa. Master Charge.

Plasteel Frames

85 COLUMBIA STREET
624-9984
HOURS: MONDAY TO FRIDAY 9:30-5:00
SATURDAY 10:00-2:00
CLOSED SATURDAY DURING SUMMER.

If you purchase a valuable piece of art from a Seattle gallery and ask about framing, chances are the recommendation will be to take it to the people at Plasteel Frames. Tom Blue, Mike Davis, Jean Stewart and Spike Hendricksen have been framing fine art for a long time and have earned a real respect for the quality of their work. Plasteel is where many of the city's artists bring their paintings, and you can imagine how exacting *their* standards are. Located in a space at the old Daily Journal of Commerce Building, they have lots of room to deal with even the largest canvases, something they do often for some of the best galleries and art collections in Seattle. The types of frames available are legion . . . from welded aluminum to plexiglas, metal section, and all kinds of hardwood frames. Plasteel can also stretch and mount canvases, and fabricate plexiglas frames and cubes to order. And, for good measure, everyone here is polite and friendly and knows what's what.
Visa. Master Charge.

Seattle Art

1816 - 8TH AVENUE
(next to Greyhound Bus Depot)
624-0711
HOURS: MONDAY-FRIDAY 8:00-5:00
SATURDAY 8:00-1:00
(Summer hours vary slightly)

Seattle Art is one of the city's oldest businesses, and it's certainly not just a store for professional artists. It's for anyone who likes to draw, paint, paste, tear, write, set type, mount photographs or frame pictures — or just wants a well-supplied studio or office. Take a poll of artists in Seattle and they'll confirm that this is where *they* find virtually everything they need for both graphic and fine art. Seattle Art has been around since 1892 and the owners know the field inside out. The inventory includes over 100,000 items . . . top-of-the-line Winsor-Newton and Grumbacher acrylic, oil and watercolor paints; graphic supplies like Artype, Formatt, Chartpak, Letraset and Geotype; drafting tools, tables, easels, light tables, block-printing and etching supplies, mat boards, canvases, acetate, carving and sculpting tools, art viewers, projectors, pens, brushes and inks. Owner Don Williams doesn't mind getting involved in a customer's project in order to provide the most complete service. Employees are well-versed in at least one of the art fields, so if one person at Seattle Art can't help you, there's another who can.
Visa. Master Charge. TransAction.

Food & Drink

Photo: Historical Society of Seattle & King County

Difficult to decide which is better: the divine "oyster light" of Seattle's sunset skies or while yumming a hot one (pan fried), that last look in an oyster-eater's eye.

Gertrude Pacific

DeLaurenti
Italian & International
Food Markets

1435 - 1ST AVENUE
PIKE PLACE MARKET
622-0141
HOURS: MONDAY-SATURDAY 9:00-6:00
317 BELLEVUE WAY N.E.
BELLEVUE
454-7155
HOURS: MONDAY-FRIDAY 10:00-6:00
SATURDAY 9:30-6:00

DeLaurenti's is the first thing most Seattleites think of when they want to visit an Italian market, but that doesn't begin to cover everything this long-established specialty food shop has to offer. They stock some of just about every kind of ethnic food you can name . . . the best brands of each one. Then there's the full-service complete deli with meats and cheeses; spicy sausages and mellow bries. After that comes the bakery, with an international flavor and great variety. Somewhere in between the two is DeLaurenti's amazing pasta section, where you can still buy your spaghetti wrapped in brown paper with a string. Upstairs holds one of the best wine, beer and mineral water selections in the city. And if all the shopping makes you hungry, you can revive yourself with a slice of pizza and an Italian ice at the take-out window. A recently opened branch in Bellevue keeps three generations of the DeLaurenti family and a terrific staff busy cutting and wrapping delicious deli treats for everyone.

The Dilettante

416 BROADWAY AVENUE E.
329-6463
HOURS: TUESDAY-THURSDAY
12 NOON-12 MIDNIGHT
FRIDAY & SATURDAY 12 NOON-1:00 AM

When we decided to do a Catalogue about the better places in town, dozens of people mentioned The Dilettante. It seems that when the subject is fine hand-dipped chocolates, the word travels fast. The story behind this place starts with a recipe that came from the kitchen of Czar Nicholas II in St.

Petersburg. Dana Taylor Davenport inherited this well-guarded secret formula from his great uncle Julius Rudolph Franzen. All this fortuitous circumstance is good news for chocolate aficionados in Seattle. The Dilettante, however, is not just a chocolate shop, but a restaurant for sweet tooths. It's open late in the evening; perfect for the dessert course of a paint-the-town progressive dinner. The ice cream sundaes are magnificent, and the rich, wonderful tortes are baked on the premises. The coffee and other non-alcoholic dessert drinks are just about as indulgent as you can imagine . . . delights such as Cocoa Caffe Deluxe, an espresso drink with Ephemere syrup. The Dilettante also sells bulk chocolate, pastries, coffee beans and chocolate chips, and it's almost impossible to leave without a few chocolates for the road.
Visa. Master Charge.

Sur La Table

78 STEWART STREET
(Across from the Market)
622-2459
HOURS: MONDAY-SATURDAY 9:30-6:00

The Pike Place Market attracts serious cooks from the whole Puget Sound region. And they come, inevitably, to stock up in the Northwest's most serious kitchen shop. Sur La Table is a comfortable, knowledgeable place where you can talk cooking, regional foods and kitchen equipment with people who know all three. There are six sizes of everything and a dozen of each size in stock and that adds up to a non-slick hardware store for the kitchen. Sur La Table stocks all models of the Cuisinart Food Processor and complete lines of Calphalon, Cuisinart, LeCreuset and Helvetia Copper so customers can see the best in aluminum, stainless steel, enameled cast iron and copper cookware side by side to decide what's best for the cooking they do. For larger kitchens and restaurants, Sur La Table sells Robot Coupes and Wolf Ranges. Along with the standard lines of cooking equipment, Sur La Table imports its own — Sabatier Jeune knives, Bourgeat fish poachers and couscousieres, and exceptional selection of baking equipment from Matfer of France and Dr. Oetker of Germany. Whether it is basic equipment at the best price or the most sophisticated equipment no one else has at all, Sur La Table is an indispensable stop for the happy cook or someone who wants to make a cook happy. Shipping and wrapping are skillfully done. Visa. Master Charge. American Express.

Starbucks
Coffee and Tea

1912 PIKE PLACE
622-8762
HOURS: MONDAY-SATURDAY 9:00-6:00

UNIVERSITY VILLAGE
522-5228
HOURS: MONDAY-FRIDAY 9:30-8:00
SATURDAY 9:30-6:00
SUNDAY 11:00-6:00

509 BROADWAY AVENUE E.
323-7888
HOURS: MONDAY-FRIDAY 9:30-9:00
SATURDAY 9:30-6:00
SUNDAY 12-6:00

10214 N.E. 8TH AVENUE
BELLEVUE 454-0191
HOURS: MONDAY-SATURDAY 9:30-6:00
SUNDAY 12-5:00

There are only two kinds of coffee . . . bad coffee and good coffee. Since Starbucks began several years ago, there has been no excuse in Seattle for bad coffee. In fact, Starbucks got started when a number of talented people decided that it was high time to pay attention to one of life's biggest little pleasures. There are other coffee stores around of course, but the clincher is that Starbucks smells the best. And the reason for *that* is because they roast the beans themselves. It's all done in the gigantic roasters down at the coffee warehouse on Airport Way. The world's finest beans go in there "green" and come out in over 20 different varieties and blends. Most are "full-city" roasted, just a few shades lighter than the dark roast preferred in Europe. Then there is all the hardware you'll find in every Starbucks shop . . . cold-water coffee makers, drip makers of all kinds, Melior pots and electric grinders. Starbucks also has an admirable selection of espresso makers, from small stove-top models through to large automatic Gaggia machines from Italy. Of course, there are more prosaic things like espresso cups, mugs, filters, infusers, tins, teapots, peanuts, chocolate and their own brand of select imported teas. Starbucks supplies coffee to 40 of Seattle's best restaurants, so you figure they're doing it right.
Visa. Master Charge.

Bud's Select Meats

202 - 106TH PLACE N.E.
BELLEVUE
454-1777
HOURS: MONDAY-SATURDAY 9:00-6:00

A rare combination of meat store, catering service and complete delicatessen, Bud's Select Meats is a classy operation. They carry a complete line of meat, including Colorado beef, aged right on the premises, chicken, turkey, veal, stuffed pork chops, and their own home-smoked pepperoni and sausage. The sausage here enjoys a reputation as the best in Seattle, and customers bring in their own game and turkey to be smoked or made into sausage at Bud's smokehouse. The deli does a booming lunch-time business with the huge variety of cold-cuts, salads and ready-made sandwiches. But the part that is really special is their complete catering department. Bud's will cater dinners from 20 to 2,000, from weddings to business openings and birthday parties. They handle every detail, from appetizers to desserts, a complete staff of bartenders and waitresses, even the flowers and decorations. There aren't many places that can diversify this much and still do everything well, but Bud's Select Meats has been doing just that for 20 years.

Mêlangeuse Bar Service

**PLEASE CALL FOR INFORMATION
364-0685**

A well-established, dependable catering service that is still small enough to keep the attention personal is a rarity. That's why Mêlangeuse, especially set up for bar service, is such a find. Owner Theresa Linvog, who learned all the fine points supervising the catering division of a large restaurant, has a devoted following in Seattle. She can create a bar service tailored to any kind of gathering or celebration . . . small birthday parties, big bashes, office functions, brunches, picnics, midnight breakfasts, weddings, lunches or whatever you can dream up. Special bar creations and wine choices can vary according to theme, and Theresa will ensure that experienced, courteous bartenders bring along all the accoutrements necessary to do it up with a flourish. Mêlangeuse is one of those wonderful combinations of an absolutely indispensible service, provided at an accessible price.

 # Wild Salmon Fish Market

**1800 W. EMERSON STREET   283-3366
HOURS: MONDAY-SATURDAY 10:00-6:00
SUNDAY 12-5:00**

The Wild Salmon Fish Market started as a fishermen's co-op, and everybody knew, of course, that they had some of the best fish in town. Now that they're a retail store they still have great fish, and more. There are tanks full of live crabs, oysters and clams (you can't get any fresher than that!), lots of other fresh and frozen seafood, as well as a complementary selection of domestic and imported wines. Specializing in troll-caught salmon, they will pack it, or any other kind of seafood, for shipment to anywhere in the world. If you are stuck for an idea on how to prepare all this delicious fare, Wild Salmon Fish Company will make suggestions or direct you to their ample collection of old and new cookbooks where you can copy any recipe that catches your fancy. Visa. Master Charge.

Uwajimaya

519 - 6TH AVENUE S.
INTERNATIONAL DISTRICT
624-6248
HOURS: MONDAY-FRIDAY 9:30-8:00
SATURDAY 9:30-6:00

N.E. 24TH & BEL-RED ROAD
BELLEVUE
747-9012
HOURS: MONDAY-FRIDAY 10:00-8:00
SATURDAY 10:00-6:00

SOUTHCENTER MALL
TUKWILA
246-7077
HOURS: MONDAY-FRIDAY 9:30-9:30
SATURDAY 9:30-6:00

Uwajimaya began 51 years ago out of the back of a truck and has grown to become Seattle's Asian supermarket. There is literally nothing else like it because it's a grocery/delicatessen/clothing store/seafood market/drugstore/gift shop/import market all rolled into one. It's all here . . . from the ordinary to the unusual, from six kinds of rice by the hundredweight to precious ginseng by the ounce. The fresh sushi and pastry counter is irresistable, and the seafood selection is the most exotic in town. Once you discover all the treats at Uwajimaya, you'll want to go back again and again — and make it a first stop when you have out of town guests. There are people who shop Uwajimaya's grocery section just because the displays are so wonderful. There are even those who've tried to dash in for a bottle of oyster sauce and an extra chopstick, but find themselves coming out with two kinds of fresh fish, some rice wine, a terrific kite, the perfect kimono and the best little bamboo steamer you ever saw.
Visa. Master Charge.

The Mexican Grocery

1912 PIKE PLACE MARKET
682-2822
HOURS: TUESDAY-SATURDAY 9:00-5:00

Downtown Seattle finally has a Mexican food shop and it's called, logically enough, The Mexican Grocery. It's located in Pike Place Market and run by Estefanita Sanchez (you can call her Steve). Among its many distinctions is the fact that it's the only place in town where you can buy "fresh-from-scratch" tortillas, made locally by La Mexicana Tortilla Factory. Any good Mexican cook knows the difference a real tortilla makes to a Mexican meal. Some of the other hard-to-find items are handmade tamales wrapped in cornhusks; chorizo, a spicy Mexican sausage, and several different varieties of dried chili pods including Ancho, Pasillo and Cascabal. There are also Mexican soft drinks, fruit juices, Mexican chocolate (best price in town!), various canned sauces and vegetables, candies and The Mexican Gorcery's very own, very spicy hot sauce. Steve is, of course, an experienced Mexican cook, so she can tell you which chilis are mild, which will take the top of your head off and so on. Whether you're an old hand at this cuisine or just learning, The Mexican Grocery is the only place to go.

 # New York
Bagel Boys

UNIVERSITY VILLAGE SHOPPING MALL
523-1340
CROSSROADS SHOPPING CENTER
BELLEVUE
641-5300
SEA-TAC PLAZA
FEDERAL WAY
941-1241
HOURS: MONDAY-FRIDAY 9:00-7:00
SATURDAY 9:00-6:00
SUNDAY 8:00-4:00
SEA-TAC CLOSED SUNDAY.

There are only two ways to get a decent, authentic kosher bagel. One is to have a sympathetic friend air mail them from Brooklyn at great expense. The other is to go to University Village, Federal Way, or Crossroad Shopping Center, and buy yourself a dozen from New York Bagel Boys. The second way is better. These are the real thing — New York water bagels baked on boards in the hearth of the oven, true to the original recipe that was discovered by owner Daniel Levi Romero from a long family line of bagel makers in New York. Whether you choose plain, sesame, poppy seed, garlic, egg or onion, you'll have to agree bagels are why cream cheese was invented. The Bagel Boys make their own terrific cream cheese, by the way, and offer lots of other great bagel fixings like lox, turkey and pastrami. You can eat them fresh or go the ''freeze-now, eat-later'' route but, in case you can't resist turning a visit here into lunch, New York Bagel Boys also carries beverages and other deli treats.

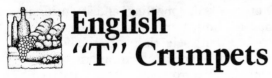 # English "T" Crumpets

PIKE PLACE MARKET
1503 1ST AVENUE
682-1598
MONDAY-FRIDAY 9:30 A.M.-5:00 P.M.
SATURDAY 9:00 A.M.-5:30 P.M.

There's something terribly comforting about a crumpet. The very word conjures up warm images of steaming tea cups in cosy drawing rooms. Whether you prefer to consume your crumpets in this idyllic setting or while strolling through Pike Place Market, English "T" Crumpets is your cup of tea. From the moment you walk in, past the largest selection of preserves on the West Coast, you just know that this place is steeped in tradition. Owner Gary Lasater got his recipe from the restaurant started over 50 years ago by Mrs. Hawthorne, Victoria's famous crumpet lady. Gary offers a choice of white or whole wheat crumpets (and a special wild rice version at Thanksgiving and Christmas) and bakes them in the window while you watch. Eat them toasted right there with your choice of butter, honey, ricotta cheese or preserves, and then buy a half-dozen to take home to comfort you on the next rainy day. Which, after all, could be tomorrow.

 # Natural Food Garden

621 BROADWAY AVENUE E., CAPITOL HILL
323-8900
4217 UNIVERSITY WAY N.E.,
UNIVERSITY DISTRICT
634-3430
HOURS: MONDAY-FRIDAY 10:00-8:00
SATURDAY & SUNDAY 10:00-6:00

The Natural Food Garden is Seattle's real food supermarket. The two locations sell only whole, unadulterated, unprocessed food . . . which means no sugar, no white flour, no chemical additives, no preservatives, no artificial colorings, and no hydrogenated oils. The Natural Food Garden is definitely not one of those too-casual places where they're always out of tofu and never give you a bag unless you specially ask. It's more like a supermarket, without the Hamburger Helper . . . and a hundred times more pleasant. Natural Food Garden is well-stocked, appealing, and attention is prompt. They sell bulk grains, beans, nuts and seeds; a complete dairy selection with the best cheese prices in town; and a full complement of organically and locally-grown produce. They also have nutritious snack products, natural fruit juices, healthy instant fare in the freezer — and welcome convenience items like paper and cleaning products to save you a second shopping trip. They also stock vitamins, natural cosmetics, and appliances like juicers and yogurt makers. If you're hungry right now, Natural Food Garden on Capitol Hill has a deli and bakery on the premises serving sandwiches, bread, muffins, and other good treats to go.
Visa. Master Charge. TransAction.

Pike Place Market Creamery

1518 PIKE PLACE
622-5029
HOURS: MONDAY-SATURDAY 9:00-6:00

The Pike Place Creamery is an udder delight. This little outdoor shop brings the farm to downtown Seattle. The Creamery's milk is fresh from local dairies and comes in glass bottles, just like the good old days. The eggs here are fresh, full of flavor and have nice chubby yolks. Owner Nancy Douty is proud that her products are all natural with no added chemicals or preservatives. Although the shop features local products, you can also find many dairy items from other parts of the country. Ice cream gourmets can count on a freezer full of Haagen-Dazs, without a doubt the best commercial ice cream available anywhere in the country. Other Pike Place Market Creamery favorites are Wagon Wheel raw milk and cream; Alta Dena yogurt, kefir and ice cream; Island Spring tofu and temph, fresh from Vashon Island; Natural Nectar ice cream sandwiches; Just Delicious rice pudding; and Wilcox sour cream. There's an ever-changing selection of special treats at the counter, like whole wheat fig bars and one-serving cheesecakes. And here's a real scoop: you can buy yourself a Haagen-Dazs ice cream T-shirt with your favorite flavor on the back.

Truffles

3701 N.E. 45TH
522-3016
HOURS: MONDAY-FRIDAY
10:00 A.M.-8:00 P.M.
SATURDAY 10:00 A.M.-6:30 P.M.

Truffles is divine. In fact, everything in this specialty grocery shop is as mouthwatering as the French delicacy for which it is named. Actually, Truffles is more like five stores in one . . . it features a full complement of bulk coffees and teas, meats, cheeses, wine, beer; carries strictly top-of-the-line gourmet cookware; and has one of the best delicatessens in town. To begin at the beginning, the coffees and teas are from the finest known sources, and a planned espresso coffee bar will offer customers on-the-spot samples. The selection of cheeses is superb . . . there are dozens of varieties, all carefully handled and sold at the peak of perfection. Beer and wine are imported from all over the world and many of these may be purchased chilled. The gourmet foods run the gamut from exotic canned, bottled and packaged French and English treats to frozen sauces and Haagen Dazs Ice Cream, sold by the dish or by the quart to go. And the deli! Just try to choose. New York corned beef, home made quiches and soups, freshly-made salads like tabouleh, ratatouille, French potato salad, New York cole slaw, an excellent chicken with curry, remoulade, or white bean and sausage. A little of each, please . . . bite for bite, you can't beat Truffles.
Visa. Master Charge.

Specialty Spice Shop

85A PIKE PLACE MARKET
622-6340

HOURS: MONDAY-SATURDAY 9:00-6:00

1937 S. SEA-TAC MALL
FEDERAL WAY, WASHINGTON
839-0922

616 TACOMA MALL
TACOMA, WASHINGTON
474-7524

HOURS: MONDAY-FRIDAY 9:30-9:30
SATURDAY 9:30-6:00
SUNDAY 12-5:00

One of the most familiar smells in the Pike Place Market is the delightful and tantalizing aroma of Market Spice Tea. If you follow your nose, you'll find the Specialty Spice Shop, where Market Spice Tea was born. Established in 1911, the shop is owned by Steve Zien and Ruby Rutelonis. Steve handles the business affairs while Ruby mixes and blends all the exotic tea and spice concoctions that have made her famous. Anyone who knows Ruby will agree that what she doesn't know about tea and spices just isn't worth knowing. She's spent a lifetime studying her craft and the amazing selection in the shop reflects it. At last count there were 2,000 kinds of bulk and packaged spices, tea, coffee, condiments, as well as tea pots and all kinds of brewing paraphernalia. Ruby airmails her special blends of tea and spices all over the world. So, if you ever find yourself in Washington, D.C. craving a cup, never fear. Even Neiman-Marcus is well-supplied with Ruby's own Market Spice Tea. Visa. Master Charge.

Mr. J's Kitchen Gourmet

10630 N.E. 8TH AVENUE
BELLEVUE
455-2270
HOURS: MONDAY-SATURDAY 10:00-5:30

Larry Jaffe, owner of Mr. J's Kitchen Gourmet, is so certain that his shop has the largest selection of cookware and dinnerware on the West Coast that he absolutely guarantees it. The shop is certainly spacious enough to accommodate such an enormous stock. It's remarkable, in fact, that so many specialty kitchen items even exist; evidence of the burgeoning popularity of home gourmet activity. Suffice to say that you'll find virtually everything you need to prepare any recipe in hand. The variety extends to dinnerware, flatware, kitchen knives, pots, pans, platters, casseroles, appliances, and a cornucopia of equipment. from the best known manufacturers . . . Arabia, Dansk, Iron Mountain, Trend Pacific, Lauffer, Chicago Cutlery, Cuisinart, Asta and Waldo. A planned expansion will double Mr. J's floor space, to accommodate a new fine china and crystal department. Something unusual for a cookware specialty shop is the terrific wine cellar, which stocks quality selections from all over the world. There is also a convenient bridal registry and a special order service. Mr. J's Kitchen Gourmet is also popular on account of its celebrity cooking classes, where well-known chefs from all over the city can show you how to make the most of all this wonderful equipment.
Visa. Master Charge.

The Wedge

4760 UNIVERSITY VILLAGE PLACE N.E.
523-2560
HOURS: MONDAY-WEDNESDAY &
SATURDAY 10:00-6:00
THURSDAY & FRIDAY 10:00-7:00
SUNDAY 12:00-5:00

The word "wedge" brings to mind cheese, and cheese is indeed what this shop in the University Village is all about. If you're the sort who always has trouble just deciding on an ice cream flavor, be advised that The Wedge carries an astounding selection of over 250 types of cheeses. However, this shop is a very hospitable place and they're happy to offer samples of any variety to help you make up your mind. In fact, we can't make up our minds which ones to list, so we'll simply go on to say The Wedge also carries many other delightful gourmet foods as well. There is fresh pate, fresh caviar, all kinds of deli meats . . . brioche, croissants and pain du chocolat delivered fresh every morning from Les Boulangers Associes; as well as breadsticks, whole grain breads, french bread, biscuits, imported beers and wines, and all manner of exotic gourmet oddments. Owner Jan Weaver and staff at The Wedge convey a camaraderie that makes shopping here a pleasure. Each customer gets personal attention whether it's to arrange for one of their custom gift packs, or just something for today's lunch. The Wedge has a complete catering service, providing cheeses, meats, pates, and appropriate wines . . . virtually everything you need to throw a great party for anywhere from 20 to 1,000 of your closest friends.

University Seafood & Poultry

UNIVERSITY WAY N.E. &
N.E. 47TH STREET
632-3900   632-3700
HOURS: MONDAY-FRIDAY 10:00-6:00
SATURDAY 9:30-5:30

The supermarket system has taken a lot of fun out of shopping and a lot of the taste out of cooking. It's difficult to get a succulent stew from frozen fish, and cellophane does nothing to enhance the flavor of fresh shrimp. Freshness is one good reason to shop European-style in Seattle, and University Seafood & Poultry is one very good place to get the best fresh fish and chicken. There's no computerized checkout counter here. Instead, you'll find dedication, personal service and only pick-of-the-catch seafood and farm-choice poultry and eggs. Owner Dale Erickson and his family handle all this prime fare expertly, from cleaning and packing to advice on recipes and preparation. Packing gift shipments is also a specialty here; they'll pack it to carry or pack it to mail. University Seafood & Poultry is one of those traditions that give a city its personality. It's no wonder people have been coming from all over to shop here for over 70 years...and from Eastern Washington, they come with ice chests!

The Yogurt Stand

1410 N.E. 43RD STREET
632-5310
HOURS: MONDAY-SATURDAY 10:00-10:00
SUNDAY 12-8:00
1207 MADISON STREET
623-5430
HOURS: MONDAY-FRIDAY 10:00-6:00
AURORA VILLAGE
1140 AURORA VILLAGE PLACE N.
542-3039
HOURS: MONDAY-FRIDAY 9:30-9:30
SATURDAY 9:30-6:00 SUNDAY 12-5:00

When you've found the Yogurt Stand, you've found the best frozen yogurt in town. They've got all these delicious flavors . . . pumpkin, egg nog, mocha, chocolate mint, raspberry, almond and coconut pineapple . . . that not only taste great but are chockfull of 3 kinds of bacteria cultures which are what makes yogurt so good for you. The atmosphere is relaxed and friendly, not at all "health-foodish", but the fare is still good-for-you stuff like homemade soup, hearty sandwiches with avocado or shrimp or even peanut butter and banana, plus yogurt pies, shakes and sundaes, fresh fruit, yogurt smoothies and a special shake with lecithin and brewer's yeast added for good measure. It's nice to know that food this rich and delicious can actually be good for you.

Pike & Western Wine Merchants

1934 PIKE PLACE
PIKE PLACE MARKET
623-1307
682-1034
HOURS: MONDAY-SATURDAY 9:30-6:00

When it's market day, and you've been to the baker, the butcher, the fishmonger, and your favorite vegetable man, the next stop should be the wine merchant. Why should a bottle of wine, fruit of the vine, be the last thing on your list? Well, there's less chance of dropping it, but more important, Pike & Western Wine Merchants is at the end of the Market , well positioned to help you finish your shopping with just the right wine to go with what you've just purchased for that special meal. This shop at the junction of Western, Virginia, and Pike Place is active, but not intimidating. There is a staff of wine enthusiasts who have a knack for making you feel like a bit of a connoisseur, whether you know anything about wine or not. You'll walk out with a selection you'll be proud to open and you won't have spent your last dime. The prices at Pike & Western are usually between $3 and $6, the well-rounded inventory of selected wines come mostly from Europe and California, but a source of true pride is the selection of Northwest wines. Pike & Western represents over 15 Pacific Northwest wineries, and this is definitely the right place for those who prefer indigenous imbibing. The owners are Ron Irvine and Jack Bagdade, M.D. Ron's wine recommendations are featured in Judy Geise's book, The Northwest Kitchen. This shop carries 15 different champagnes and an excellent selection of beers and ciders. If you can't make it to the market, Pike & Western will deliver anywhere downtown for a small fee. Wine may be the last thing on your list, but at Pike & Western, it won't be just an afterthought.
Visa. Master Charge.

Woerne's European Pastry Shop and Restaurant

4108 UNIVERSITY WAY N.E.
632-7893
HOURS: TUESDAY-SATURDAY 9:00-6:00
CLOSED SUNDAY AND MONDAY

Students have been sharing sweet memories of Woerne's for twenty years. This genuine European bakery is one of the oldest, most popular establishments in the University District, and one whiff explains why. Woerne's is a pastry paradise filled with the aroma of Black Forest cherry cake, wedding cakes, Danishes and Black Forest bread fresh from the oven. There are no preservatives, no stabilizers and no imitations here. In fact, most of the recipes were brought from Germany by owner Guenther Woerne. Guenther was the first in Seattle to introduce the European idea of a pastry shop where people could sit to enjoy their sweets, teas or coffee. Over the years, the entire Woerne family has worked to make the idea a success. Today, Woerne's serves more than pastries. There are genuine German lunches of Jagdwurst, Killbasa and Berliner Bratswurst, as well as salads and quiches. There's also a unique selection of German wines from Guenther's home region of Baden. To old and new customers alike, Woerne's will always be a quiet atmosphere in which to meet friends and enjoy a taste of Europe.
Visa. Master Charge.

Theatre & Dance

Photo: Historical Society of Seattle & King County

The basic element holding this city together is the notion that there exists here a special quality of life well worth hanging on to.

Charles Royer

 # Seattle Repertory Theatre

**BOX OFFICE: 225 MERCER, SEATTLE
447-4764
HOURS: TUESDAY-SATURDAY
12:00 NOON-8:30 P.M.
SUNDAY 4:20 P.M.-7:30 P.M.
ADMINISTRATIVE OFFICE:
CENTER HOUSE, SEATTLE CENTER
447-4730
HOURS: MONDAY-FRIDAY 9:00-5:00**

The Seattle Repertory Theatre is nationally recognized as one of the country's leading professional theatres, dedicated to presenting outstanding contemporary plays, established classics and promising new works. During its six-play season the Rep assembles the finest directors, designers, artists, and actors from Seattle and throughout the country to create first rate, lively entertainment for this city's discriminating audiences. Since the Rep opened its doors in 1963, more than 3 million have enjoyed SRT productions. The Rep's 17th season are Shaw's Saint Joan, A History of the American Film by Christopher Durang, Ibsen's prophetic work, "An Enemy of the People", Shakespeare's "The Taming of the Shrew", "Spokesong" by Stewart Parker, Broadway's adult musical "Pal Joey". Consulting Artistic Director is John Hirsh, Producing Director Peter Donnelly, Resident Director Daniel Sullivan and Associate Director Richard Gershman. The Seattle Repertory Theatre is happy to provide information about tickets and season subscriptions; call 447-4764 or 447-4730.
Visa. Master Charge. Frederick & Nelson.

Photo: Chris Bennion

Cecelia Riddett & Denis Arndt in
Simon Gray's "Otherwise Engaged" (July '79)

A Contemporary Theatre

**100 W. ROY STREET
BOX OFFICE: 285-5110
HOURS: 12 NOON-8:00 P.M. EXCEPT MONDAY
OFFICE: 285-3220
HOURS: MONDAY-FRIDAY
9:00 A.M.-5:30 P.M.**

A Contemporary Theatre, better known around the city as ACT, was established in 1965 and is a leading company among quality professional theatres in Seattle. In fifteen years, ACT has presented more than 100 productions that were seen by over a million people. Presenting a good mixture of the adventurous and the traditional, the theatre has sponsored dozens of world, American and west coast premieres, many of them plays which received Tony Awards, Obies and Pulitzer Prizes. ACT is where Seattle audiences first saw professional productions of Albee, Beckett, Ionesco, Pinter, Stoppard as well as many other contemporary playwrights. In addition to the 6-show Mainstage season, running from May through October, ACT offers an annual Christmas show and a new professional children's production each year. ACT is a member of the League of Resident Theatres, is in the upper 20% of all American non-profit theatres in size, and is recognized as one of Seattle's six major cultural institutions.
Visa. Master Charge. American Express. Carte Blanche.

Photo: Chris Bennion

Intiman Theatre Company

P.O. BOX 4246
SEATTLE, WASHINGTON 98104
624-4541
BOX OFFICE 447-4651
PERFORMING AT THE 2ND STAGE
THEATRE.
1419 - 8TH AVENUE

Intiman is a professional resident theatre company founded in 1972 by its present artistic director, Margaret Booker. This company provides play-goers with an intimate theatre experience. The seating capacity is limited to 340, to help achieve a personal interaction between audience and performer. The repertoire focuses on classics and modern masterpieces, ranging from Greek tragedies such as "Medea" to contemporary dramas like "Moon for the Misbegotten." Actors in the resident ensemble company are given the opportunity to play many different roles, exhibiting the widest possible range of their artistic capabilities. Intiman presents a series of five plays, from June through October, at The 2nd Stage Theatre on 8th Avenue between Pike and Union Streets in downtown Seattle. Most tickets are sold on a series basis, offering a 20% discount to season subscribers, but are also available on an individual basis through the box office. For information about plays, schedule, subscriptions and ticket availability, call the theatre.
Visa. Master Charge.

Seattle Theatre Arts

6600 FIRST AVENUE N.E.
524-2722, 524-5543
HOURS: MONDAY-SATURDAY
10:00 A.M.-10:00 P.M.

All the world's a stage and all the men and women, adults or children, beginning, intermediate, advanced or professional level, are merely players at Seattle Theatre Arts in the Greenlake area. It's a non-profit theatre training institute which developed out of a need in Seattle for non-academic dramatic training taught by top theatre professionals. They teach all levels of acting, plus the art of auditioning, applied Shakespeare, vocal production, musical theatre, voice, mime, dialects, directing, tap, jazz, modern, and folk dancing. They have a full curriculum for teenagers and children. In addition Seattle Theatre Arts is the executive producer for the Phoenix Players, a company of actors and theatre technicians, 50 years and older. The Radost Folk Ensemble, 45 professional dancers, musicians and singers who perform Balkan and traditional American arts, and are also an integral part of the institute.
Visa. Master Charge.

The Empty Space

919 E. PIKE STREET
BOX OFFICE 325-4443
HOURS: TUESDAY-SUNDAY 2:00-6:00
ADMINISTRATION 325-4444
MONDAY-FRIDAY 9:00-6:00

The Empty Space is a theatre company of special significance in Seattle. It is certainly one of the most talked about, and deservedly so. The Empty Space has introduced more new playwrights and talented actors to Seattle than any other company. Its innovative, exciting productions have drawn nationwide attention, particularly for premiers of work by David Mamet, George Walker and Pulitzer Prize winner Sam Shepard. Founded in 1970, the Empty Space conducts an 11-month season divided into four different programs. The Mainstage Season includes 6 or 7 professional productions, chiefly new works. The New Playwright's Forum provides staged readings and workshop productions of plays in progress, with audience interaction. Fast-paced, highly theatrical, even outrageous projects characterize the Midnight Theatre, featuring everything from experimental theatre to cabaret shows. The fourth area of endeavour has been a Seattle tradition for 7 years . . . in which the talents of the Empty Space Theatre are shown free to people in parks all over the city.
Visa. Master Charge.

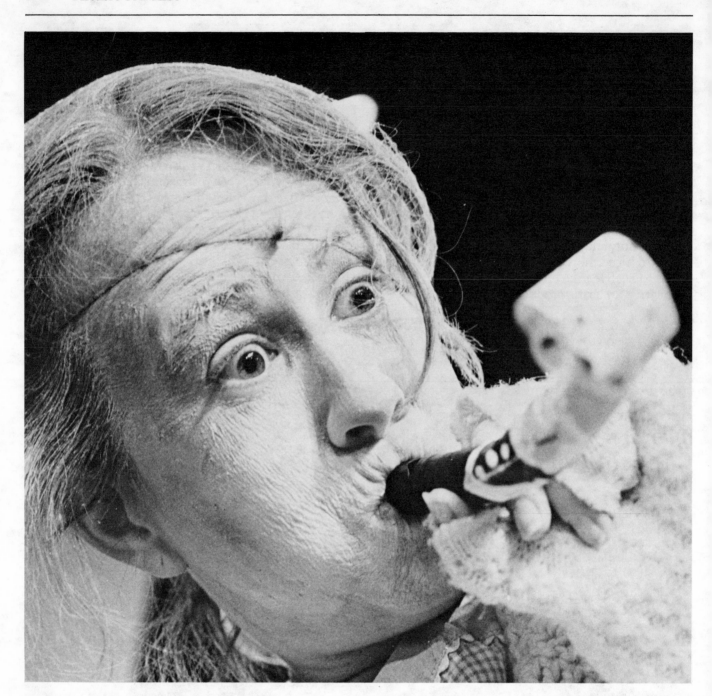

The Bathhouse Theatre

7312 W. GREENLAKE DRIVE N.
524-9110
CALL FOR TICKET RESERVATIONS AND INFORMATION.

The Bathhouse Theatre, on the northwest shore of Greenlake, has very quickly grown from a thriving community group to one of the most successful theatre companies in Seattle. Its home is a building that used to be a bath house for Greenlake, remodeled for the theatre in 1969. Since 1978, The Bathhouse Theatre has been concentrating on the production of new plays, including a number of American and west coast premieres, as well as revivals of seldom-produced works. Last year's exemplary season included David Mamet's ''Life in the Theatre'', ''Les Belles Soeurs'' by French-Canadian playwright Michel Tremblay, ''Bay City Blues'' adapted by Seattle actor Robert Wright, and Syd Cheatle's ''Straight Up''. For information on schedules and season tickets, telephone the theatre office.

Poncho Theatre

100 DEXTER AVE. N. (office)
50TH & FREMONT, WOODLAND PARK
ZOO (box office)
633-4567
HOURS: MONDAY-SATURDAY 8:30-5:30

Television . . . watch out! There *are* alternatives and the Poncho Theatre is an addictive one for both children and adults. The theatre is a division of the Seattle Department of Parks and Recreation, and it's located just inside the entrance to the Woodland Park Zoo. This theatre is seen as a model around the county because of its pleasant environment. The children have close contact with the stage and the fantasy world depicted there. The productions entertain, challenge, and invite the audience to enter the lives of the characters. Poncho Theatre is actively participating in creating a new realm of children's theatre. Their fresh productions include To Kill a Mockingbird, Huckleberry Finn, and The Boy Talked to Whales. This is where kids and adults can enjoy the spark of culture. Poncho Theatre produces a continuing film series four times a year on Monday evenings. Free showings are also offered on Monday afternoons for senior citizens only. Drama classes for children grades 3 through 12 are taught all year round in 8-week sessions. For scheduling information and admission prices for films, classes, and the theatre season, call the Poncho Theatre office.

Pacific Northwest Ballet

GOOD SHEPHARD CENTER
4649 SUNNYSIDE AVE. NO.
447-4751
TICKETS/INFORMATION: 447-4655

The Pacific Northwest Ballet is a young company but this fine classical ballet troupe has become enormously popular in just six years. In fact, their annual Christmas production of the Nutcracker performed with the Seattle Symphony Orchestra is one of the best-attended cultural traditions in the city. Every year, the company adds new performances to its repertorial history, and each new performance is always a sell-out. The Pacific Northwest Ballet has won this reputation by its strong, lively style, a commitment to showcasing the work of young, innovative choreographers, and an admirable command of the ballet classics. Enthusiasm shines through every new undertaking. The Pacific Northwest Ballet subscription season covers 16 performances of the Nutcracker, 4 other productions during the year, and a full schedule of master-level classes in classical ballet, demonstrations, open rehearsals and special performances for art openings and private gatherings. The 1979-80 season will present the world premiere performance of a work choreographed by the company's artistic director Ken Stowell, works by George Balanchine and Tchaikovsky, Benjamin Harkarvy and Vivaldi, Charles Czarny and Handel, as well as a world premiere of a ballet created by noted choreographer, Choo San Goh.

The Bill Evans Dance Company

sponsored by Dance Theatre Seattle

704 - 19TH AVENUE E.
322-3733
OFFICE OPEN MONDAY-FRIDAY 9:00-5:00
CLASSES VARY IN TIMES.
PERFORMANCES VARY IN TIMES.

The Bill Evans Dance Company is an ensemble of 10 talented modern dancers who also happen to be exceptional teachers. The company is sponsored by Dance Theatre Seattle, and was established when Mr. Evans came here from the Utah Repertory Dance Theatre in 1976. It has quickly become one of the most popular companies in the city. Bill Evans' choreography ranges from light-hearted irreverence to profound drama, and Seattleites have responded enthusiastically from the beginning. The Company presents 4 major performing seasons here each year, and also conducts a very energetic national tour schedule. This year they will be dancing at the Kennedy Center for the Performing Arts in Washington, D.C. They also find time to tour the state and are devoting more and more attention to activities in Seattle, where teaching is an important focus. The Bill Evans Dance Company provides a solid curriculum that both the serious student of modern dance and those with recreation in mind should know about. For information about the Dance Theatre School, telephone them.
Visa. Master Charge.

Photo: Gulacsik

Dorothy Fisher Ballet Center

9715 FIRDALE AVENUE
EDMONDS, WASHINGTON 98020
(206) 546-1657
For information about classes and
performances, please telephone.

Dorothy Fisher, a pioneer in the dance world in the Northwest, has been director of the Dorothy Fisher Ballet Center in Seattle for nearly 40 years. Ably assisted by choreographer Nelle Fisher, teacher and choreographer Blake Little and teacher Judy Ross, the Center has produced dancers for such reknowned companies as the American Ballet Theatre, Stuttgart Ballet, Alvin Ailey, Agnes De Mille's Heritage Ballet, Dennis Wayne's Dancers and Ballet West. Both private and class lessons are available. General ballet lessons are designed to develop the technique of the student, and perfect the technique of the accomplished dancer. Performances are an important part of learning ballet, and all students are invited to participate in an event that winds up the school year. Students who display special talent and desire are also asked to join the Dorothy Fisher Concert Dancers, who perform several times a year in Seattle and around the Northwest. A member of the National Association for Regional Ballet and a charter member of the Pacific Regional Ballet Association, the Dorothy Fisher Ballet Center is a leading participant in the festivals held every year by these groups.

 **Repertory Dancers
Northwest/Pacific
Dance Center**

**1214 - 10TH AVENUE
324-4397**

Repertory Dancers Northwest is a vital new dance company with strong roots in Seattle's dance community. Artistic Director Phyllis Legters is founder and former director of Dance Theatre Seattle and a director of Pacific Dance Center, the teaching arm of this company. Her vision of a professional dance company encompasses the ability to present recognized masterpieces of the modern dance repertoire, combined with a willingness to create and present new and experimental works. Repertory Dancers Northwest is well on its way to realizing that vision. Made up of talented, experienced dancers, the company is deeply committed to performing. It has presented concerts at Seattle University, was featured at the opening of the new Broadway Auditorium at Seattle Central Community College and has provided public programs sponsored by the King County Arts Commission. Through the teaching facilities at Pacific Dance Theatre, this non-profit organization conducts professional classes for serious students of ballet and the Graham technique of modern dance, as well as classes for people interested in studying dance simply for the love of it.

Music & Entertainment

Photo: Historical Society of Seattle & King County

The bluest skies you've ever seen are in Seattle.

Perry Como

 # Seattle Symphony Orchestra

**305 HARRISON STREET
SEATTLE
447-4700**

The Seattle Symphony had its first opening night in 1903. It is the oldest cultural institution in the Pacific Northwest. It is certainly one of the most popular, and since the arrival of Rainer Miedél, the symphony's exciting conductor, its popularity has grown tremendously. Presenting a full complement of concerts, the symphony season provides something for everyone. In addition to the regular subscription concerts, there are many special programs. One example is the Sunday matinee, ''Stars of the Future Series.'' This is a showcase for young artists on their way to becoming international performers. World-renowned artists such as Beverly Sills, Leontyne Price, Van Cliburn and Artur Rubinstein are featured with the symphony in special concerts and recitals. The Seattle Symphony is one of the few orchestras in the country employing a full-time staff for its educational programs. It presents Family Concerts in communities outside the Seattle area, a music appreciation program in the public schools called ''Musical Keys'', plus Saturday morning concerts and the popular Miedél at Meany series. The Poncho Pops Concerts are another yearly presentation. The Seattle Symphony Chorale, for four years the offical choral arm of the Symphony, gives an added dimension to the chorale programing. Its repertoire includes Handel's *Messiah*, Verdi's *Requiem*, Orff's *Carmina Burana*, and Bach's *Christmas Oratorio*. 1980 is the year of the Symphony's first European tour, a major step in the development of the orchestra and one which will enhance Seattle's image abroad.

Philadelphia String Quartet

UNIVERSITY OF WASHINGTON LECTURES & CONCERTS
MEANY HALL AB 10 (TICKETS)
UNIVERSITY OF WASHINGTON
206-543-4880
HOURS: MONDAY-FRIDAY 8:00-5:00
BOX OFFICE OPEN ONE HOUR PRIOR TO CONCERT

Seattle's own Philadelphia String Quartet is one of the Northwest's cultural treasures. It was formed in 1960 under the sponsorship of the Philadelphia Symphony Orchestra, but moved west 14 years ago to accept the title "Artist-in-Residence" at the University of Washington. The Quartet's four members have lived in Seattle ever since. They present seven regular concerts here every year, which usually take place in Meany Hall. In between, they tour extensively. Cities throughout the Northwest make up much of their itinerary, but the Quartet has performed all over the world, always winning unqualified acclaim for the beauty and depth of their music. A book could be written to relate the events of their international travels. Belfast, for example, remembers them as the first American group to visit there in many years. They braved much controversy and danger to win the admiration and love of people there. At home, these four virtuosos — Carter Enyeart, Irwin Eisenberg, Alan Iglitzin and Stanley Ritchie — appear at many other events, like the annual Beethoven Quartet cycle, and collaborate in concert with other performing groups. Listening to the Philadelphia String Quartet is a special experience, attributable to their profound musicianship, ensemble perfection, and the warmth of their sound.

 **Parnell's**

313 OCCIDENTAL MALL
624-2387
HOURS: MONDAY 11:30 AM-3:00 PM
FOR LUNCH ONLY.
TUESDAY-THURSDAY 11:30 AM-1:00 AM
FRIDAY 11:30 AM-1:30 AM
SATURDAY 1:00 PM-1:30 AM
SUNDAY 6:30 PM-1:00 AM

Parnell's is the best jazz club in Seattle. It's the only place where you can hear the world's finest jazz musicians, choose from a wonderful selection of beer and wine by the bottle or glass, and enjoy delicious Greek-inspired cuisine on top of it all. This place would be popular if it only did one of these things well, but it is testimony to Roy Parnell's dedication and energy that the club excels in all three. It's warm and comfortable, an atmosphere people immediately feel at home in. There's lots of room to lean back and relax, the lighting is subdued . . . the perfect situation for listening to fine jazz. Among the greats who have not only performed there, but asked to be invited back are: Milt Jackson, Earl "Fatha" Hines, Dexter Gordon, Kenny Burrell, Herb Ellis, Cal Tjader, Sonny Stitt and lots more. Talented locals like Jane Lambert and Gary Peacock also make frequent appearances. Parnell's is also a popular lunchtime spot . . . outside on Occidental Mall during fine weather or inside where you can enjoy the best in recorded jazz.

Northwest Chamber Orchestra

119 S. MAIN
624-6595
HOURS 9:00-4:30
Concerts presented at:
Seattle Concert Theatre
1153 John Street
624-2770

There are only a handful of professional chamber orchestras in the entire country, and Seattle has one of distinction. Currently enjoying its seventh season, the Northwest Chamber Orchestra plays an important part in the cultural life of our city. The group is made up of a core of fourteen members and each year they play host to guest artists from all over the world. Jean Francois Paillard, Karl Richter, James Galway, and Elly Ameling have all enhanced the reputation of the Northwest Chamber Orchestra throughout the country. A Bach Festival, A Baroque Festival, and performances with the Bill Evans Dance Company are other highlights in their history. The Orchestra performs regularly for schools and senior citizens in addition to the usual concert season, which comprises eight subscription concerts. Most of these are staged at the Seattle Concert Theatre where a natural shell provides favorable acoustics and an intimate atmosphere. Additional concerts brighten the Christmas season and special events like the Imagination series are held.

 # Seattle Opera

The Opera House at Seattle Center

P.O. BOX 9248
447-4711 TICKET OFFICE
447-4700 ADMIN/ARTISTIC OFFICE
HOURS: MONDAY-FRIDAY 10:00-4:00

Our pioneers certainly believed in Seattle's potential, but little did they know that by 1980 one of the biggest attractions bringing new faces this far north and west would be the Opera. The Seattle Opera was established in just 1964. It's one of the

Photo: Chris Bennion

youngest opera companies in the country, but thanks to a contemporary pioneer, director Glynn Ross, this company now ranks in the top six nationally. It has gained world-wide respect for it's Pacific Northwest Wagner Festival. Ours is the only Festival in the world to present the entire four-opera cycle, the Ring of the Nibelung, in both German and English every summer. The Seattle Opera measures up to such a challenge. They've been setting trends ever since 1966 when they became the first company to present a regular series of performances in English featuring a group of rising young American artists in addition to performances of each opera in the original language with stars of international reknown. Traditional favorites, rare or unusual works, premieres of operas by 20th century American composers, are all in the range of regular opera season performances, which is made up of five operas, each with six performances. Stars the stature of Pavarotti, Scotto, Carreras, and Nilsson are featured in special performances with the Opera company. The year long Singers Training Program nurtures undiscovered talents, and other progressive programs focus on educational outreach. There are programs for students and adults with touring shows, previews, and community performances. Ticket prices cover a broad spectrum, making Opera an experience accessible to everyone.

 Seattle Chamber Singers

**1605 17TH AVENUE
SEATTLE, WA 98122
(TICKET INFORMATION)**

The Seattle Chamber Singers started as a madrigal group 10 years ago. The warm response from the city's music lovers encouraged them to expand their ranks, add instrumental accompaniment, and begin to perform oratorios. Their successes include exciting performances of Bach's "Mass in B Minor", Handel's "Messiah" and many other Baroque oratorios and choral compositions. Musical director and founder, George Shangrow conducts the Seattle Chamber Singers with an enthusiasm and flair that is delightful to watch. He has earned critical acclaim throughout the Northwest and Europe both for his conducting skills and his performances on harpsichord and piano. The season includes regularly scheduled oratorios throughout the year, as well as special programs like the Connoisseur Choral concerts. These highlight a range of music from turn-of-the-century French art songs or long respected Italian masses and even American Barbershop Quartet music. Concerts are held at a variety of locations...Meany Hall at the University of Washington, the Broadway Auditorium at Seattle Central Community College, and various churches in the area. Tickets are available individually or at a savings in series packages.

Seattle Brass Ensemble

9709 ROOSEVELT WAY N.E.
524-0431
784-7118
HOURS: MONDAY-FRIDAY
8:00 A.M.-11:00 P.M.

Why is music such a difficult thing to decide on when you're planning an occasion? Because it's important. The nicest setting, the most spectacular catering can be quite drab without some musical life . . . enter the horn. The Seattle Brass Ensemble deserves a fanfare. This chamber music group, a non profit organization, has served Seattle well. Their repertoire ranges from Renaissance and Baroque to contemporary music. Formal concerts are impressive and often include new works by Northwest composers. They commission 2 or 3 original pieces a year from composers such as Alan Hovhaness, William O. Smith, Ronald Neal Jones, Daniel Davis, and Paul Carmona. The Seattle Brass Ensemble plays at churches, weddings, funerals, schools, parks, and good-time concerts. They can even perk up a party with ragtime, or provide the right touch of class to a holiday celebration. No partridge or pear tree, but two trumpets, one French horn, one trombone, and one bass trombone, make up the ensemble. For special events the group is joined by Paul Reitz on the pipe organ. The Seattle Brass Ensemble travels extensively on concert tours throughout the Northwest, and since the past year their home for regular concerts is the delightful Seattle Concert Theatre.

Lectures & Concerts

**MEANY HALL
OFFICE AB-10
AT THE UNIVERSITY OF
WASHINGTON
543-4880**

With an exciting assortment of cultural presentations, Lectures & Concerts is one of Seattle's greatest resources for leisure time activities. Most events are presented in comfortable Meany Hall. The theme is quality entertainment and lots of it. Music is a major focus . . . the International Chamber Music Series, which features the most distinguished chamber ensembles from around the world; School of Music faculty recitals, opera productions and the faculty wind quintet, Soni Ventorum; concerts by the Philadelphia String Quartet, now in residence at the University of Washington; plus lively special attractions such as the Canadian Brass. Dance performances are equally popular . . . evenings devoted to the University of Washington Dance Theatre and the annual Independent Choreographers Showcase. Lectures & Concerts is a major sponsor of the Discover Dance series, which presents America's most exciting touring ballet and modern dance companies. Lectures & Concerts also presents "Super Saturday", a family program of films, mime shows and musical ensembles. To get your name on the mailing list for a monthly calendar of events, or to find out what's happening this weekend, call Lectures & Concerts at 543-4880.

Seattle Pro Musica

6205 LATONA AVENUE N.E.

525-8294

Seattle Pro Musica was founded in 1973 by current musical director Richard Sparks. The organization consists of 3 groups. The Pro Musica Singers and Pro Musica Chamber Orchestra are top-rated amateur ensembles whose repertoires include selections ranging from Renaissance music to 20th century compositions. Together, these two groups have presented Mozart's C Minor Mass, Haydn's Harmoniemesse, Bach's St. Matthew and St. John Passions. The orchestra has also performed Mozart's G Minor Symphony and D Minor Concerto, Beethoven's 1st Symphony and many other works. The third group, the Bach Ensemble, is composed of professional performers, 12 singers and 15 instrumentalists. Using actual period instruments or replicas, this ensemble specializes in Baroque music. During their concert season, they frequently present special performances with other Seattle groups, such as the Duo Geminiani. Single tickets and subscriptions are available in advance.

Pike Place Cinema

1428 POST AVENUE IN SEATTLE'S PUBLIC MARKET 622-2552

Photo: Nick Jahn

TICKETS:
$3.50 GENERAL ADMISSION
$3.00 SEATTLE FILM SOCIETY MEMBERS
$2.00 GROUPS OF 20 OR MORE
$1.50 SENIOR CITIZENS & CHILDREN

The smaller, independent specialty movie houses seem to do well in Seattle, thanks to enthusiastic support from the film-loving community, and to the efforts of theatres like Pike Place Cinema to provide quality entertainment. Pike Place Cinema is the first independent cinema to crop up in downtown Seattle, and is located at the foot of Pike Street next to Le Bistro Restaurant. It's a brand new 300-seat house committed to showing quality first-run films from the United States and abroad. They also bring in American film revivals, film retrospectives, and schedule weekday luncheon matinees, weekend children's matinees and showcase the work of Northwest independent filmmakers. The lobby is one of the nicest in town, which is where you'll find the refreshment stand. They have fresh pastries, juices, imported chocolates, natural snacks and, of course, popcorn with real butter. That's the delightful bonus . . . quality treats to go with quality celluloid at Pike Place Cinema.

Seattle Concert Theatre

1153 JOHN STREET 624-2770

Located in a beautiful old renovated building, the Seattle Concert Theatre is probably the most unusual concert facility in Seattle. It represents very well how precious old buildings can be injected with life in response to community need. Holding as many as 375 people, the Seattle Concert Theatre puts its ideal size, excellent acoustics and large reception area to good use hosting such diverse activities as chamber music, jazz, solo recitals, folk festivals, classic films, and dramatic productions. The family of popular concert hall users include the Northwest Chamber Orchestra, Musica Viva Chamber Players, Early Music Guild, Seattle Brass Ensemble, Au-Roar Productions, Seattle Pro Musica, Seattle Classic Guitar Society, Pacific Lively Arts, Magic Penny Productions, and the Seattle Film Society. Call the office for rental or event information.

David Saunders
Violin Makers & Dealers

405 WEST GALER ST.
283-5566
HOURS: MONDAY-FRIDAY
10:00-5:00
SATURDAY
10:00 A.M.-4:00 P.M.
JULY-AUG. —
10:00 A.M.-2:00 P.M.

Real craftsmen, the kind who invest years of time, energy and study in the perfection of their art, are a rare breed. David Saunders, violin-maker, is such a craftsman. Mr. Saunders repairs and restores fine old violins, violas and cellos as well as handcrafting new. His customers come from far and near, either to buy from his excellent collection, or to avail themselves of his highly regarded repair work. The shop's international reputation attracts many visiting musicians who need emergency repairs. His followers are also the teachers, students and professional musicians and artists who have developed close ties to the shop over the years.

David Saunders dispenses advice on maintenance and care of old musical instruments, demonstrates techniques that he and his staff use in the shop. Although the sign above the door says "Violin Maker", this exacting and time-consuming process can only be carried on as time permits. Just looking at these fine hand-crafted instruments is music to the eyes. Violin cases and accessories are available at the shop as well; in fact this is one of the best sources in the city. Mr. Saunders is a member of the Appraisers Association of America and provides an appraisal service of old and rare violins.

 # Mt. Olympus Imports

231 S.W. 152ND ST.
244-4419
HOURS: MONDAY-FRIDAY 12:00-8:00
SATURDAY 11:00-7:00

Mt. Olympus Imports dates its roots back to the British rock invasion 15 years ago, when Americans first became aware of the superior quality of European-made recordings. Those are the roots . . . the shop actually has only been open a year but already they've gained a solid reputation as a leading retail and mail-order import record store in the city. The staff are dedicated musicologists who can guide you expertly through this excellent selection. Mt. Olympus carries lots of classical labels with special emphasis on HMV, British Decca, Digital, and Direct Disc productions. They boast the best collection of Japanese pressings in the U.S. The different types of music available on imports is impressive . . . popular rock artists, reggae, new wave, heavy metal, avant-garde, jazz, folk, and electronic music. Imported records cost more because of their quality, so Mt. Olympus believes a customer should be able to listen to an album before purchasing it. Accordingly, the store has two turntables and headphone sets available. If you don't see a record in stock, please ask. Mt. Olympus, with their connections, will locate it for you. If you don't have time to visit in person, please call to take advantage of their excellent worldwide mail-order service.
Visa. Master Charge.

 # The Fifth Avenue Record Shop

**1301 5TH AVENUE
RAINIER SQUARE
624-6507
HOURS: MONDAY-SATURDAY 9:30-6:00**

The Fifth Avenue Record Shop kept its original name even after it moved from the street location to the Rainier Square concourse, because it is, after all, the same store, only bigger and better. This shop has kept a reputation for Seattle's best classical and jazz record selection since 1940, and now they have three times the space to accommodate an even wider selection. The Fifth Avenue Record Shop has an excellent group of film sound track albums from Broadway shows, international and import releases, and a very respectable collection of pop and rock albums. They feature tapes as well . . . open reel, cassette and 8-track . . . and a complete supply of record care accessories. The sales staff are all musically-educated and very helpful. If they can't locate an album for you, they'll make every effort to have it special-ordered. Fifth Avenue Records also publishes and mails a bi-monthly newsletter, offering information about new releases, developments in the recording industry and advance notice of sales at the store.

Visa. Master Charge. American Express.

Johnson-West Music Service

500 DENNY WAY
682-6883
CALL TOLL-FREE FROM ANYWHERE IN
WASHINGTON 1-800-732-1103
CALL TOLL-FREE FROM ANYWHERE
OUT-OF-STATE 1-800-426-9904

Doug and Joy Corbin, owners of Johnson-West, have always been involved in the world of music. Both hold degrees in music from the University of Southern California and they owned a successful music store in Los Angeles for 15 years before moving to Seattle. Putting all this experience to work, they set out to compile the largest and finest selection of classical, school and choral music in Seattle. They have more than succeeded — in fact, Johnson-West enjoys a world-wide reputation for their music collection. This store carries detailed scores for every instrument in the orchestra, plus an equally comprehensive selection of scores for school bands, stage bands, and classical chamber groups. Choral arrangements are available in a wide range of subjects for church and school groups or professional chorales. The collection of music for solo instruments and performances is outstanding. Johnson-West carries contemporary jazz charts and some popular music as well. They will special order any score in print for you and provide mail order service all over the world.

Definitive Audio

6017 ROOSEVELT WAY N.E.
524-6633
HOURS: TUESDAY-FRIDAY
12:00 NOON-8:00 P.M.
SATURDAY 11:00 A.M.-7:00 P.M.
SUNDAY 12:00 A.M.-5:00 P.M.

Great strides have been made in the record business since the days of the Ink Spots, even since Jimmy Hendrix. The top groups and recording artists have been getting closer and closer to studio quality on the albums released. Definitive Audio specializes in stereo systems that maximize that quality. It is a high-end audio store, featuring state-of-the-art high-fidelity equipment. The owners are Jay Huber and James Croft, and the theme they have established for this audio inventory is musicality . . . equipment that intensifies the perception and accuracy of the music. Definitive Audio sells complete systems from $600. They provide free installation and set up, placing and adjusting to make sure the customer gets the optimum musicality from a new system. There's an in-house service department, and out of consideration for those who love to enhance their leisure time with music, but can't shop during the week, Definitive Audio is open on Sundays.
Visa. Master Charge.

The Guitar Center

8TH & VIRGINIA
623-8877
HOURS: MONDAY 10:00 AM-9:00 PM
TUESDAY-THURSDAY 10:00 AM-7:00 PM
FRIDAY 10:00 AM-9:00 PM
SATURDAY 10:00 AM-6:00 PM
SUNDAY 12 NOON-6:00 PM

The Guitar Center in Seattle is the music store professionals depend on. The people who work here have been around Seattle long enough to be familiar with the music scene, and give great personalized service to professional and amateur music people alike. There are over 600 guitars, banjos, mandolins and dobros, so you're sure to find exactly what you need. In fact, the Guitar Center is virtually wall-to-wall guitars, both electric and acoustic, manufactured by the best names the world over . . . Fender, Gibson, Guild, Martin, Ovation, Washburn and many others. The featured lines of amps include Acoustic, Altec, BGW, DBX, EV, JBL, Kustom, Marshall, MXR, Tapco and Tangent. This store is also Seattle's largest drum outlet and carries drum sets and cymbals by all the major manufacturers, as well as a well-stocked supply of sticks, drum heads and other percussion necessities. Keyboard players will find the finest and most advanced synthesizer technology from Crumar, Fender, Moog, Rhodes and Roland. This doesn't even begin to cover the selection, which also includes microphones, instrument cases, guitar parts and more. Professionals like Led Zeppelin, Heart and The Moody Blues have depended on the Guitar Center for quality products because this place has it all. Visa. Master Charge. Financing available.

The Magic Flute Music & Stereo

709 WESTLAKE N.
682-2340
HOURS: MONDAY-SATURDAY 10:00-6:00

The Magic Flute Music & Stereo store numbers among its patrons the employees of other music and stereo stores in the Northwest. The reason for this disloyalty is prices that represent such a savings, usually 40%-50%, they beat most discounts. The Magic Flute specializes in used, reconditioned, and new close-out models of musical instruments and stereo components of every conceivable make and model. They also have a limited number of new items where demand requires. Their stock comes direct from wholesalers and manufacturers as well as from the public, but they sell a large number of instruments on a consignment program. That means you've just found the perfect place to sell that beautiful bassoon in your son's closet under the tennis rackets and water skis, your violin that never learned to read music, or the stereo system you've finally outgrown. They manage to sell virtually everything that comes in . . . if it makes music, the Magic Flute has not only sold it, but they've probably got two more stashed in the back. This is definitely the place to visit first, if you want to save time, trouble, and money.
Visa. Master Charge.

 # Jack McGovern's Music Hall

7TH AND OLIVE
SEATTLE
TICKET OFFICE: 682-9333
EXECUTIVE OFFICE: 292-9449

Located in the beautifully restored 1929 Fox Theatre, Jack McGovern's Music Hall has brought to Seattle the best of big-time entertainment. The renovation boasts 1½ million dollars of renewed opulence . . . an elegant backdrop to current top name artists such as Rosemary Clooney and the Mills Brothers. Seattle residents have particularly lost their hearts to Julie Miller, McGovern's multi-talented resident star, whose energetic impersonations of the grand ladies of show business have played to rave reviews. Stars abound here, including the dazzle and glitter of the Jo Emery Dancers, the David Jackson singers, and the high-stepping Follies girls, along with host Don Martin who perform original musical revues nightly. For 90 minutes of non-stop, high-energy entertainment, and spectacular special effects à la Vegas, put on the ritz and enjoy an elegant evening, complete with dinner and cocktails, at the Music Hall. Reservations are recommended; large groups are gladly accommodated.

 ## Goldie's on Broadway

1509 BROADWAY AVENUE
324-4656
HOURS: MONDAY 6:30 p.m.-2:00 a.m.
TUESDAY-SATURDAY 11:00 a.m.-2:00 a.m.

Goldie's is where live rock and roll happens on Capitol Hill. They have a big dance floor, which is fortunate because this club always draws a big crowd. There's a large raised stage, for good views from almost anywhere in the place. For those who are not crazy about rug-cutting and jumping around to the band, Goldie's has provided plenty of pool tables, pinball machines and video games. The entertainment ranges back and forth between local and national acts, showcasing the best music and musical styles in the country. During a typical month at Goldie's, you'll hear everything from a big-time country/rock band, to local rock and roll (like the sizzling hot Heaters pictured above), or maybe some 50's style rockabilly or a nationally known jazz group. There's more than just the usual bar food here too. Lunches feature a variety of steaks, burgers and fish and chips with your favorite beer, wine or soft drinks on the side.

Restaurants

Photo: Historical Society of Seattle & King County

Ain't there any Mannings Cafeterias in Washington? They got them all over Florida.

Tourist in Seattle taxicab

Mikado

514 S. JACKSON STREET
622-5206
HOURS: MONDAY-SATURDAY
5:30 P.M.-10:00 P.M.

Even if it didn't already have the reputation as the most elegant and attractive Japanese restaurant in Seattle, Mikado would be worth visiting for the quality and freshness of its seafood alone. It's no secret that this restaurant gets the pick of Seattle's bountiful seafood catch everyday. The mouth-watering sushi or fresh grilled robatayaki proves it, along with delicate crab, salmon, oysters, and prawns, Mikado style. There's more than one way to experience the pleasure of dining here. The informal sushi and robatayaki bars invite spontaneity, while the family style dinners are formal, perfectly attended, but leisurely. The art of traditional Japanese cuisine is practised at Mikado. You can select from beef, chicken, and seafood teriyaki, or crisp, perfectly dipped tempura, plus sukiyaki or taban-yaki prepared at your table, and various kinds and sashimi. The a la carte menu is extensive, including many delicious tofu dishes, sushi, fish roe, and soups. For a special occasion, the ceremony of the Mikado Kaiseki Dinner, served in the traditional Japanese manner, is wonderful. Telephone in advance to arrange parties and consult with the chef about special selections. Private tatami rooms are available for parties of five or more. Validated parking is available at Sea-First across the street.
Visa. Master Charge. American Express.

Le Tastevin

**501 QUEEN ANNE AVE. N.
SEATTLE
283-0991
HOURS: TUESDAY-FRIDAY
11:30-2:30 — LUNCH
MONDAY-SATURDAY 5:00-10:30 DINNER**

Le Tastevin is a great French restaurant, and, to many Seattle diners, it's quietly a singular favorite. It may be that this mysterious "low profile" quality is what makes this personable place so delightful. The cuisine is directed by chef and co-owner Jacques Boiroux, who has created a thoroughly original menu that combines classic French dishes with his own special flair. Several of his own recipes involve the use of our fresh local seafood. Thus, you'll find Duckling with Calvados sauce, a fragrant Boullabaise Puget Sound, delicate salmon dishes and other seasonal specialties, keeping company with classical continental interpretations of veal and beef entrees. The wine selection here is easily one of the best in the city, attended by co-owner Emile Ninaud who is a leading wine merchant and enologist. There is something remarkable enough about the atmosphere and service at Le Tastevin that makes it perfect for a spontaneous mid-week visit, a convenient dinner before the Opera or the Symphony, or the ideal choice for a special celebration. If you're feeling informal, you'll fit right in. But if it's a noteworthy night, every grand expectation will be met, from the first sip of wine to the last bite of Le Tastevin's exquisite homemade French pastry.
Visa. Master Charge.

Gerard's
Relais de Lyon

17121 BOTHELL WAY N.E.
485-7600
HOURS: TUESDAY-SUNDAY
5:00 P.M.-11:00 P.M.

Housed in a charming old brick mansion in Bothell, Gerard's Relais de Lyon recreates the tradition of fine old French provincial inns. Lyon is a region in France, famous for the rich cream and butter so essential to French cooking in "haute" style. Gerard's Relais de Lyon is a tribute to the region and elegant French cuisine. Born and raised in France, chef Gerard Parrat studied with master chef Paul Bocuse, and runs his restaurant according to the time-honored European tradition where diners are treated with care and courtesy. The menu at Gerard's changes seasonally. This gives the chef a chance to demonstrate his expertise in many ways with the freshest ingredients, and it provides diversity for the many people who dine often at Gerard's. The atmosphere is elegant and comfortable with a warm, intimate feeling. During the week, any of the rooms can be used for private parties, and special meals for such occasions can be arranged in advance. A comprehensive wine list and fresh homemade pastries complement an evening of first class dining at Gerard's.

Visa. Master Charge. Diners Club.

Deville's on Broadway

1833 BROADWAY AVENUE E.
325-5392
HOURS: MONDAY-FRIDAY 11:30-2:30
5:30-10:00
SATURDAY AND SUNDAY 5:30-11:00

Michel Deville is getting rave reviews on Broadway with this new brasserie. The reason is a sensational combination of "la cuisine bourgeoise" served at what are virtually bargain prices, and terrific service. The menu offers the best of everyday French cuisine . . . just like Mama used to cook for supper every evening in Paris. It includes freshly made soup from market vegetables, crepes stuffed with the best Puget Sound sole and salmon, and omelettes rich with truffles, the black gold of France. Michel Deville has been a well-known Seattle-area chef for years, launching the cuisine for several successful restaurants, including The Mirabeau in Seattle and his own "Michel's" in Des Moines. His reputation reaches new heights at Deville's on Broadway. Temptation begins right at the front door with a dessert display that varies from sinfully rich eclairs to heavenly almond cake in a puff pastry. Mama never cooked like this!
Visa. Master Charge. BankAmericard. American Express.

Annique's

2037 SIXTH AVENUE AT LENORA
624-6434
HOURS:
LUNCH: MONDAY-FRIDAY 11:00-2:30
DINNER: MONDAY-THURSDAY 5:30-10:00
FRIDAY-SATURDAY 5:30-11:00
MONDAY-FRIDAY 5:00-7:00
COMPLIMENTARY HORS D'OEUVRES

Le Pate de Foies de Volalille au Cognac . . . how's that for a starter? Fowl liver pate in cognac, snails in garlic parsley butter, marinated mussels — these are some of "Les Hors D'Oeuvre" from the menu at Annique's, where classical French cuisine may be enjoyed in an elegant 18th Century setting. Dinner is served like a well-constructed play, and the hors d'oeuvre open the show. So, be prepared to spend the evening and enjoy a leisurely meal from vichyssoise to mousse chocolat. The owners, Annick and Guy Myhre, started in the restaurant business in France in 1959. They have brought to Seattle experience, pride, and favorite family recipes from the Normandy region of France. The mid-day meal is shown great respect at Annique's. The menu and service at lunch are designed to meet any budget, diet, or schedule. There's the Express French combination for those in a hurry; health dishes without sugar, salt, oils, and fat for those on a diet, a multi-course lunch for the leisurely; and a variety of salads and other specials. Annique's also offers a special catering service. The main dining room holds up to 120 people, and is available for meetings, banquets, weddings, receptions, even dinner dances. The catering menu ranges from a simple, but delightful French breakfast, to a multi-course gourmet dinner. They are happy to cater parties at your own home. If you would like to serve hors d'oeuvre which truly deserve their French name, have Annique's take care of your next party. For this distinctive catering service, call 624-2296. Visa. Master Charge. Diners Club.

Le Provençal

**212 CENTRAL WAY
KIRKLAND, WASHINGTON
827-3300
HOURS: MONDAY-SATURDAY
5:30 P.M.-11:00 P.M.
RESERVATIONS NECESSARY ON
WEEKENDS.**

A taste of the French countryside pervades the charming Le Provençal in Kirkland. People return here again and again to savor some of the best veal and rack of lamb west of Avignon. They are never disappointed. Owner Philippe Gayte grew up in the kitchen — his parents own a restaurant in France — and the restaurant business is all he's ever known. It's his belief that many French restaurants do not last long because the owner has to work, work, work. But Philippe himself thrives on it. He seems to be everywhere at once, supervising the chef's cooking and working as maître d'. Philippe has worked at the world famous Le Pavilion in New York and Ernie's in San Francisco, an experience that has evidently paid off at his own Le Provençal. The food and service are consistently good; the selection of wines excellent. And one more plus here — the parking is free.
Visa. Master Charge. American Express. Diners Club.

The Mirabeau

**46TH FLOOR,
SEATTLE FIRST BANK
BUILDING
624-4550
HOURS: LUNCH:
MONDAY-FRIDAY
11:30 A.M.-2:30 P.M.
DINNER:
MONDAY-SATURDAY
5:30-10:30 P.M.
BAR OPEN 'TILL 1 A.M.
WEEKDAYS AND
2:00 A.M. WEEKENDS**

The Mirabeau, located at the top of the Seattle First National Bank Building, is known for outstanding continental cuisine, flawless service, and a panoramic view of the city and Puget Sound. One of Seattle's favorite restaurants, the Mirabeau is also recognized around the country, and has been awarded top honors in the selective diner's guide, Where to Eat in America. All the dishes at the Mirabeau are prepared with Northwest products. You'll want to take your time with the menu. It's impressive and selective, full of inviting specialties . . . and the spectacular scenery is a relaxing reminder that there's never any rush in a restaurant of this class. If you know what you want in advance — in fact, if you caught it yourself — the chef at the Mirabeau will prepare your fish or game to exact specifications, with advance notice. You'll find the selection of accompanying wines to be another pleasant diversion. The list is long and the vintages are well-chosen. The bar at the Mirabeau is elegant and always well-populated, and after sunset the view gets better and better.

Visa. Master Charge. American Express.

Maximilien in the Market

**IN THE CORNER OF PIKE PLACE MARKET
AT THE END OF PIKE STREET
682-7270
HOURS: MONDAY-WEDNESDAY
7:30 A.M.-5:30 P.M.
THURSDAY, FRIDAY, SATURDAY
7:30 A.M.-10:00 P.M.**

Maximilien in the Market is the newest venture of successful restaurateur Francois Kissel. The food, service and atmosphere at Maximilien measure up fully to the high standards set by his other two places . . . this one, the perfect expression of its Pike Place Market location. It's open for breakfast, lunch and dinner, so patrons may enjoy the marvelous Puget Sound view, morning, noon and night. Breakfast comes continental with espresso coffee; crusty, buttery croissants and other morning pastries — or full-course if you prefer, with Maximilien's own daily souffle. At lunchtime, the service is cafeteria-style, which allows you to view the impressive array of salads, soups, meat or fish dishes before choosing. The full-service dinner menu boasts a delicious variety of starters, entrees and wonderful desserts that all make the most of the produce, fish and other specialty foods available at the public market. The atmosphere at Maximilien is particularly inviting during the evening, when the nighttime panorama of Elliott Bay is the complimentary course to every meal.
Visa. Master Charge. American Express.

Cafe Sabika

**315 E. PINE STREET
622-3272
DINNER ONLY
HOURS: TUESDAY-
SATURDAY 5:30-10:00**

Dining at Cafe Sabika is like going to a friend's house for dinner . . . only we all should have friends who cook this well. It's an intimate and comfortable place; the menu is ambitious, yet unpretentious, and best of all, the preparation is impeccable. Cafe Sabika has a Mediterranean flavor, and offers Italian, Spanish and French dishes. Chef/owner Collins Jones begins the day at Pike Place Market to collect the ingredients of his seasonal menu, which changes every month. Some of his notable specialties are escalopes de veau, bouillabaise, paella and various pasta dishes. Desserts are unusual and delicious; the wine and beer selection is very respectable. Cafe Sabika is small and popular and open for dinner only, so calling ahead is recommended.
Visa. Master Charge.

City Loan Pavillon

206 - 1ST AVENUE S.
ENTRANCE ON OCCIDENTAL PARK
624-9970
HOURS: MONDAY-FRIDAY
11:00 A.M.-11:00 P.M.
SATURDAY-SUNDAY 4:00 P.M.-11:00 P.M.

The glass walls and ceiling of the City Loan Pavillon claim a little piece of Occidental Park in Pioneer Square that gives this restaurant a greenhouse feeling in warm weather, and, in Seattle's drizzly season, allows diners to enjoy the rhythm of the rain while savoring the delicious fare prepared in this first-rate Seattle Kitchen. The menu reads French, but the descriptions, like "George Washington cherry mousse", indicate that owner Francois Kissel has given his second-born restaurant a culinary personality that links two continents. There is a full selection of courses comprised of some two dozen entrees, many of which offer unexpected combinations . . . like Crevettes Caussoise, a preparation in which prawns are sauteed with cucumbers in a creamy blue cheese sauce; Liver Noumea, done with avocado, onions, lemon and crushed peanuts; or a classic carrot cake topped with homemade chocolate sauce and candied carrots. If it's not unusual, it's elegantly simple . . . like the selection of fresh, lightly-dressed salads or a New York steak, pan-fried with mustard butter. The decor is handsomely appointed with authentic 17th and 18th Century furnishings . . . and the enormous golden crystal chandelier suggests an opulent counterpoint to the vignettes of urban life in the square just outside.
Visa. Master Charge. American Express.

Brasserie Pittsbourg

602-1ST AVENUE
623-4167
HOURS: MONDAY-SATURDAY 11:30-2:30
FOR LUNCH
MONDAY-THURSDAY 5:30-10:30
FRIDAY & SATURDAY 5:30-11:30

The success of the Pioneer Square redevelopment owes a great deal to a wonderful, well-loved restaurant that Seattleites call "the Brasserie". People discovered the Brasserie Pittsbourg and went on to explore the entire district. The Brasserie was the first of three restaurants created by Francois Kissel, unquestionably one of our region's best classically trained Parisian chefs; and wife Julia, a native Seattleite. Ironically, the Brasserie adds a unique dimension to life in this city partly because you feel you've *left* the city to take a meal in a Paris quartier. Down the stairs, just below street level, your introduction to the Brasserie is a steamy blast of fragrant tarragon. Indeed, chicken tarragon is one excellent choice from this admirable French menu. But if you can resist that appealing combination, you'll do just as well with Canard a l'Orange, Boeuf Bourguignon, or medallions of veal so tender you can cut them with a fork. And every day, one of several kinds of the special Brasserie omelette is offered. Luncheon is a refreshingly simplified proposition where the choice is from a few select dishes, quickly served in cafeteria fashion. Table service at dinner is attentive; the "linen" is the classic butcher paper of a true French brasserie. The Brasserie Pittsbourg also has a charming private dining room, in a French provincial decor, which may be served for gatherings of up to 50 people. Visa. Master Charge. American Express.

Le Bistro

**93A PIKE STREET
IN POST ALLEY, PIKE PLACE MARKET
682-3049
HOURS: MONDAY-SATURDAY
11:00 AM-2:00 AM**

A city needs to have achieved a certain degree of sophistication for restaurants like Le Bistro to exist. First come all those grand places that huff and puff and carry on, and when all that blows over, places like Le Bistro arrive. The menu, the wine list, the service and the decor have an assurance that doesn't need to be asserted; it's just there. Located at the foot of Pike Street in the Public Market, Le Bistro is an elegant and comfortable place to dine, from lunchtime until late in the evening. The white walls, archways and warm lighting impart a nice, unhurried Mediterranean flavor. The handwritten menu takes up just one page, is divided simply into appetizers and entrees, and includes antipasto, prawns, pasta, cioppino, veal dishes and a dinner special each evening. Open until 11 p.m. on Friday and Saturday nights, Le Bistro is one of the very few places in Seattle to go for a good late dinner. The "after hours" menu features antipasto, prawns aglio and della casa, fettuccine, pasta with two kinds of clam sauce, pasta marinara, bistro steak, excellent desserts, espresso coffee and a good choice of cognacs. Also part of the late-night scene, the bar at Le Bistro is wonderful and unquestionably one of the best in Seattle.

Visa. Master Charge. American Express.

Henry's
off Broadway

1705 E. OLIVE WAY, CAPITOL HILL
329-8063
HOURS:
DAILY 11:00 A.M.-2:00 A.M.
SUNDAY BRUNCH 10:00 A.M.-2:00 P.M.
RESERVATIONS SUGGESTED
OYSTER BAR - ALL HOURS

Ask a number of people to name the most elegant restaurant in town, and most of them will immediately say "Henry's off Broadway". It is unabashedly chic inside and out . . . from the landscaped terrace entrance with valet parking service, to the beautiful bar and dining room with deep-green plush mohair banquettes and hand-painted murals and elaborate furnishings throughout. All this sets the mood for special treatment, and indeed, the service is outstanding. It's inviting, smooth and pleasant from reception to departure. This kind of flair doesn't come together by accident. The owners spent 2 years and over $1 million to ensure that Henry's would be a unique restaurant experience for Seattle. During its 2-year history, the cuisine here has come to command the same admiration as the lovely atmosphere. The menu offers an array of dishes to please even the most discriminating tastes . . . Rack of Lamb Dijon, Veal Scallopini Marsala and Abalone Doré Amandine are among the house specialties; the salads and desserts are impressive, and there's an especially complete list of appetizers. The Oyster Bar is one of the most popular after-work and late-night spots in town, and a great alternative for those who prefer to sample one or two appetizer dishes such as Angels on Horseback, Escargot, Scampi ala Henry's and Deep-Fried Zuchinni rather than opt for a full dinner. Henry's has it all . . . in the poshest surroundings since "The Great Gatsby". Visa. Master Charge. American Express. TransAction.

The America's Cup

**MARINERS SQUARE
1900 N. NORTHLAKE WAY
633-0161
HOURS: LUNCH:
MONDAY-SATURDAY
11:00 A.M.-3:00 P.M.
DINNER:
SUNDAY-THURSDAY
4:30 PM-11:30 PM
FRIDAY & SATURDAY
4:30 PM-12:30 PM
SUNDAY BRUNCH:
9:30 AM-2:30 PM**

The America's Cup is the achievement of well-known Seattle restaurateur, Peter Huwiler, who believes that to be great, a restaurant must provide three things . . . quality food, good service and the best possible atmosphere. The America's Cup measures high on all counts. In fact, the theme of this restaurant, its setting and its menu are uniquely harmonious, inspired by the century-old U.S. sailing challenge cup. The architecture and interior decor are superb, along with the wonderful view of the Ship Canal, Lake Union and the Seattle skyline. That's reason enough to take in a meal at The America's Cup. The food, however, will keep you coming back. The America's Cup features entrees from five different countries: France, Sweden, England, Australia and the United States. The menu ranges from the exotic to the familiar; from a hearty prime rib platter or corned beef and cabbage, to a delicate scallops Veronique. All entrees are accompanied by fresh vegetables, excellently prepared. Even the most familiar dishes are done up with unusual and imaginative touches. Service is pleasant; families are welcome and everyone will enjoy the spacious, understated elegance.

Visa. Master Charge. American Express. Diners Club.

The Broadway Restaurant

314 BROADWAY AVENUE E.
323-1990
LUNCH, DINNER AND BRUNCH ON
SATURDAY AND SUNDAY
HOURS: MONDAY-SATURDAY
11:30 AM-2:00 AM
SUNDAY 10:00 AM-2:00 AM

The Broadway Restaurant is a very popular place. The owners maintain that it's a restaurant first and a bar second, but the truth is that they're very successful at both. There are three distinct atmospheres; each has its own attractions. The New York style bar is just what it should be . . . a magnetic, uptempo and crowded night-spot for sleek city people; yet low-key and comfortable for weekend brunches with the newspaper spread out on the bar. The skylit Palm Court offers dining in a cheerful and airy setting with tall plants arching over your table. Just a step away, but a world apart, is the Club Room. It's elegant, intimate and warmly decorated by a draping tent ceiling, where you can well imagine yourself in an exotic desert hideaway-scene from a Rudolph Valentino movie. What all three rooms have in common is the consistently fine cuisine . . . rendered from the Broadway's dedication to taking the freshest possible food and doing as little as necessary to it, for the palate's full appreciation. Once you've tried one of the select entrees, many of them unique to the Broadway, you'll find that this philosophy is on the mark. The wine cellar is likewise an important part of this restaurant's smooth service, and stocks almost 400 selections. There is always a long list of fresh desserts, including a marvelous chocolate sundae, brought in by special arrangement from The Dilettante just down the street. Reservations are recommended, and a valet parking service is available.
Visa. Master Charge. American Express.

Ray's Boathouse

6049 SEAVIEW AVE. N.W.
789-3770
HOURS:
LUNCH: MONDAY-FRIDAY
11:30 A.M.-3:00 P.M.
SATURDAY BAR LUNCH
12:00 P.M.-1:00 A.M.
DINNER: MONDAY-SUNDAY
5:00 P.M.-11:00 P.M.
BAR: MONDAY-FRIDAY
11:30 A.M.-2:00 A.M.
SATURDAY 12:00 A.M.-2:00 A.M.
SUNDAY 4:00 P.M.-2:00 A.M.

If you're hungry for spectacular sunsets and fresh seafood, come to Ray's Boathouse. Ray's has perched on the edge of Puget Sound for nearly 40 years, and it's still one of the hottest restaurants in Seattle today. All the things that are wonderful about living in Seattle are reflected here. Ray's serves the best of the Northwest's fresh seafood, and prepares it in delicious and imaginative ways, from elegantly simple prawns served in butter and garlic, to a rich, spicy seafood soup. The menu includes a variety of other entrees too, ranging from Tenderloin Steak and Rack of Lamb to hearty salads. Meals are complemented by an excellent wine list, featuring some of the finest local and domestic labels, as well as great European vintages. Ray's is great for salmon, and you can taste their several versions at Ray's Oasis in Boise, Idaho or Ray's Seafood Restaurant in Honolulu. The exceptionally personable staff makes dining pleasant. But, to many, it's the bar at the Shilshole Ray's that really counts. It's beautifully decorated, with a tasty hors d'oeuvre counter and a balcony with front row seats to watch the boats go by and the sun go down behind the Olympics. Ray's Oasis, Boise, Idaho (208) 342-0700; Ray's Seafood Restaurant, Honolulu, Hawaii (808) 923-5717.
Visa. Master Charge. American Express. Diners Club.

Duke's

236 - 1ST AVENUE W.
283-4400

10116 N.E. 8TH STREET
BELLEVUE
455-5775

HOURS: MONDAY-FRIDAY
11:30 AM-2:00 AM
SATURDAY & SUNDAY 5:30 PM-2:00 AM

Duke's opened up on Queen Anne Hill in 1977 and became an overnight success. The combination of quality food and drink, an adventurous menu and a flair for the contemporary that is uniquely Duke's had a lot to do with that success. Of course, the fact that the comfortable bar is always filled with interesting and attractive people hasn't hurt either. One of the few places of its calibre both on Queen Anne Hill and in Bellevue, Duke's is a great spot to see and be seen. Some people regard the terrific food as just a bonus; others come regularly out of curiosity to see which intriguing dishes are on the specials board this week. The menu is designed to accommodate every appetite; so they don't mind a bit if you've decided to pass up their elegant full-course dinners and only want to sample an appetizer or vegetable dish. It's all scrupulously fresh, simply prepared and served with despatch. The wine list at Duke's is a sophisticated distillation of the best domestic and imported varieties and covers a wide price range. The wonderful desserts come in outrageous portions, and give you a chance to linger over coffee, and watch for local celebrities who have a habit of dropping in for a taste of Duke's casual hospitality. Visa. Master Charge. American Express.

Boondock's, Sundecker's & Greenthumb's

611 BROADWAY AVENUE E.
323-7272
HOURS: MONDAY-THURSDAY
11:00 AM-3:00 AM
FRIDAY 11:00 AM-4:00 AM
SATURDAY 9:00 AM-4:00 AM
SUNDAY 9:00 AM-2:00 AM

It usually takes years to establish a tradition, but Boondock's, Sundecker's and Greenthumb's has become one in just six years. When Gerry Kingen first opened this place, the Broadway district was merely a nice little Capitol Hill retail area. Now it's one of the most entertaining dining and shopping spots in the city, and Boondock's deserves a vote of thanks for its contribution to that remarkable transition. If imitation is the highest form of flattery, then this place must indeed be envied by a score of other Seattle restaurants who have tried to duplicate its success. So far, no contest . . . Boondock's still reigns supreme as the original. The decor is casually elegant, with lots of greenery, skylights, Italian tile tables, fresh flowers always, and candlelight at night. The menu is a 20-page wonder, and all you have to do is identify the chapter that matches your appetite. They have everything from lobster to cream cheese sandwiches with avocado and tomato. The emphasis is on saute cooking, using lots of crisp, fresh vegetables, the finest seafood and an array of other ingredients that go into Boondock's famous specialty concoctions. The wine list is impressive and covers a wide price range. But what makes this place really special is the scene that has developed around it. Open until 3 a.m. it's a late-night favorite for theatre-goers, performers and people who work in other restaurants . . . who always know the best places to eat.
Visa. Master Charge. American Express.

F.X. McRory's

419 OCCIDENTAL AVE. S.
625-9818
HOURS: MONDAY-SUNDAY
5:00 P.M.-2:00 A.M.

What kind of restaurant has a complimentary phone in the lobby . . . a popular one. F.X. McRory's Steak, Chop & Oyster House is one of those busy restaurants where you don't even mind waiting a spell in the bar before dining, because the good feeling is contagious and the oysters delicious. McRory's is just a punt away from the Kingdome and it seems to be a place of constant celebration. An NBA title, a Seahawk win, or St. Patrick's Day are notable occasions here, but McRory's does not rely on special events to attract an enthusiastic clientele. They have 100 different varieties of brew, even a local or two; the world's largest collection of bourbon, yes, Old Weller's here; and the McRory shot tips up 3/8ths beyond the ounce. The stand-up oyster bar has put Seattle in the big leagues with other spots made famous by pushing aphrodisiacs on ice . . . the Oyster Bar in Grand Central Station and Felix's in New Orleans. Oysters McRory sounds like a daring dandy of the 1890's, but it's really one of the entrees. Oysters also come Rockefeller, Rosellini, fresh in the half-shell or loaded up in the stew. An eye-opening offering from their dinner menu is a 20-ounce steak, the New York Chop, a strip loin beef chop broiled with the bone for exceptional flavor. All the beef and lamb at McRory's has been locker aged for 21 days to enhance the flavor and tenderness. After-dinner is not forgotten here, and if it's vintage you want, there's turn of the century cognac, plus a recipe for McRory's bourbon coffee, a house speciality to rival the Irish at Jake's O'Shaughessy's. There's no rivalry really . . . same owners . . . same nice touch. Visa. Master Charge.

The Butcher

**300 - 120TH N.E.
(BENAROYA BUSINESS PARK)
BELLEVUE, WASHINGTON 98005
455-3930**

**5701 SIXTH AVE. S.
(BENAROYA BUSINESS PARK)
SEATTLE, WASHINGTON 98108
763-2215**

**HOURS: LUNCH — MONDAY-FRIDAY
11:15 A.M.-2:30 P.M.
DINNER — MONDAY-THURSDAY
5:30 P.M.-10:00 P.M.
FRIDAY-SATURDAY 5:30 P.M.-11:00 P.M.
SUNDAY 5:00 P.M.-10:00 P.M.
HAPPY HOUR — MONDAY-FRIDAY
4:00 P.M. - 7:00 P.M.
COMPLEMENTARY HORS D'OEUVRES**

If Isaac Newton were alive he'd probably frequent the Butcher Restaurants. He could sit under a tree and discuss business with his contemporaries or just privately ponder in the Atrium of the Seattle Butcher or the Greenhouse of the Bellevue Butcher. The Northwest is not an area known for sidewalk cafes or open air restaurants in the park, but The Butchers take the atmosphere of both, protected from the rain and cold. The tree-lined, glass-roofed interiors are a relief from stuffy offices for the business communities and the two locations are especially favorite luncheon spots. At dinner their excellent cuts of steak and prime rib will convince you that the restaurant is well-named, but their menu includes other inviting entrees such as delicate Teriyaki Chicken Breasts, Crab Stuffed Red Snapper, The Butcher Fettucini, and Pacific Northwest Salmon broiled to perfection. You can get creative at the salad bar which is famous as one of the first restaurants to come up with the idea. Don't forget dessert . . . from classic Cheesecake or fresh Strawberries Devonshire (in season) to elegant Chocolate Mousse. If you're planning a special occasion, the Atrium of the Seattle Butcher may be reserved for private parties such as company banquets, fund-raising auctions, class reunions, celebrations, fashion shows or seminars, easily handling from 30 to 900 people.
Visa. Master Charge. American Express. TransAction.

Domani

604 BELLEVUE WAY N.E.
454-4405
HOURS: MONDAY-SATURDAY LUNCH
11:00-2:30
DINNER FROM 5:30-11:30
SEVEN DAYS A WEEK

Domani has always been a marvelous space to dine, with superb Italian-inspired cuisine and beautiful surroundings. A recent remodeling, however, has added even more space, with a garden room for dining and a brand new wine bar, which offers wine by the glass and fine cheeses. The skylights and profuse greenery impart a fresh, pleasant atmosphere that seems ideally suited to the menu. Featuring a diverse array of entrees, Domani has a special flair for pasta: from fettucine to lasagne, perfectly prepared. There are four delicious chicken dishes, including Chicken Oscar and Chicken Parmigiana, a fine seafood selection, steaks and a mouthwatering array of seven different veal entrees, rendered from top quality milk-fed Provimi veal. For those who have trouble choosing, Domani offers six interesting combination meals, composed of steak alongside a sampling from other entrees. The lunchtime menu at Domani is equally good. The sandwiches and a variety of egg dishes . . . omelettes, quiche lorraine and frittatas . . . are popular daily specials here. Prices are very reasonable, ranging from $4 to $6 for lunch and $5 to $12 for dinner.
Visa. Master Charge. American Express.

McCormick's Fish House & Bar

4TH AND COLUMBIA
682-3900
HOURS: MONDAY-THURSDAY
11:00 A.M.-11:00 P.M.
FRIDAY 11:00 A.M.-MIDNIGHT
SATURDAY 5:00 P.M.-MIDNIGHT
SUNDAY 5:00 P.M.-10:00 P.M.

Bill McCormick decided to create one of the most appealing and traditional fish houses in the nation. He selected the historic former Oakland Hotel in downtown Seattle for his site. Using his imaginative sense of design, he fashioned a restaurant rich with mahogany, oak, maple, pressed tin, brass, stained glass, tile and a host of eclectic wall pieces reflecting America's heritage. To this setting he added a friendly, attentive staff and launched a menu which boasts over 40 fish entrees. The result is one of Seattle's most popular restaurants, a place known to hold the essence of any famous fish house — fresh fish. A blackboard at the front entrance of McCormick's tells the whole story . . . it lists the fresh fish for the day. At this writing, these are items on that board: Cherrystone Clams, King Salmon, Bluepoint Oysters, Eastern Scallops, Petrale Sole, Swordfish, Red Snapper, Trout, Pacific Oysters, Dungeness Crab, Clams, Sturgeon, Mussels, Atlantic Lobster (live), Seabass, Haddock and Mahimahi.
All major credit cards.

Trattoria Mitchelli

84 YESLER WAY
623-3883
HOURS: MONDAY-FRIDAY 7:00-4:00
SATURDAY 8:00-4:00
SUNDAY 11:00-8:00

Trattoria Mitchelli is one of those restaurants that become such a fixture in your life that you can date your existence by it. You *know* there was life before Mitchelli, but you can't imagine what it was like. People don't just eat at this place, they frequent it. Part of the reason it's so entertaining is that the scene keeps changing all day long. In the early morning over a big plate of eggs and homefries, it's quiet, warm and relaxing. By lunchtime, the place is so crowded you can make friends with the person on your left, read the New York Times in front of the woman across the counter and make a deal with the guy on your right to trade half his meatball sandwich for half your pasta with clam sauce, all at once. Dinner is busy and friendly, with lots of wine, good music, delicious pasta and some unique veal dishes you can write home to Mama about. But the nicest time at the Trattoria is probably midnight to 4 a.m. when the real regulars hang out, drinking espresso, eating sausage and eggs and whiling the night away. At times like that, you absolutely cannot remember what you did before Trattoria Michelli.
Visa. Master Charge.

Vaersgo

2200 N.W. MARKET STREET
782-8286
HOURS: MONDAY-SATURDAY
LUNCH 11:00-3:00
DINNER 5:30-10:30

No featured group of Seattle restaurants would be complete without one that reflects the area's strong Scandinavian heritage. Vaersgo is a fine example of the charm this culture has contributed to the city. "Vaersgo" is the traditional call to the table in Denmark, and this new restaurant extends a fine Danish hospitality from Ballard, the heart of Seattle's Scandinavian community. Owner Pat Clausen has created a well-explained, well-prepared and delicious cuisine that has won many regular patrons in a very short time. The luncheon specialties, tempting side dishes, starters and dinner entrees are as pleasing to the palate as they are to the eye. The colorful symmetry of Scandinavian food makes it very visually appealing. The same inimitable style shows up in the clean-lined Scandinavian approach to design in the broad sense . . . and incidentally, in Vaersgo's lovely, spacious decor. Similarly, the elegance of all the cuisine here is in its simplicity and freshness, a style that belies the culinary skill it takes to achieve.
Visa. Master Charge.

raison d'être

113 VIRGINIA
624-4622
HOURS: MONDAY-SATURDAY 7:00-6:00
OPEN SOME FRIDAY AND SATURDAY
EVENINGS; PLEASE CALL TO CONFIRM.

Raison d'être is the home of Seattle's busiest espresso machine. It works virtually non-stop from 7 o'clock in the morning, six days a week, and turns out a classic cappuccino along with all the other traditional bistro beverages. The steady stream of devotees who frequent this place would probably agree that if it's been a tough day in the big city, you can at least stop at raison for a cup of coffee that makes up for it all. The excellence here is attributable to a combination of the best machinery, fresh-roasted Starbucks beans, and a preparation savvy to rival the fare in downtown Rome. Coffee *is* the raison d'être, but there's much more. In fact, continental breakfast lovers never had it so good . . . a honey-drizzled cafe au lait is even better with a plate of croissants and brioche (easily Seattle's finest), baked on the premises and served hot with preserves and whipped butter. Fresh citrus juices are made to order; squeezed the hard way, section by section, for a superior texture. Lunchtime offers a variety of delicious daily specials, which are usually light enough to leave room for a raison d'être dessert. A sophisticated coffee bar like this is a sure sign of urban progress. The smooth service, exquisite decor and terrific view of Puget Sound are all quite unnecessary, but you'll just have to make do.

Copacabana Restaurant

1520½ PIKE PLACE MARKET
622-6359
HOURS: LUNCH: MONDAY-FRIDAY
11:30 AM-3:00 PM
DINNER: WEDNESDAY, THURSDAY,
FRIDAY 5:30 PM-10:00 PM
SATURDAY 11:30 AM-5:30 PM

One of the nicest dining spots in the Pike Place Market is the Copacabana, where the specialty is authentic South American food. This restaurant was opened in 1964 by Ramon and Hortensia Palaez who came to Seattle from Bolivia. Now located upstairs in the Triangle Building, it is owned by the Palaez's daughter and son-in-law Martha and Mike Morrow, who have continued her parents' native style of Latin cuisine. The Copacabana serves fine food at reasonable prices without a lot of fuss. The lunch menu features some very interesting dishes that have grown to be the real Copacabana favorites: a light appetizing green salad, spicy Saltenas, Huminta (a corn pie topped with cheese), a piquantly rich shrimp soup that is a Palaez original and a meal in itself. For dinner, there's a great paella, a traditional Bolivian chicken dish called Sajta de Pollo, baked halibut, or beef tongue done up in a thick and zesty sauce. Beverage choices include a good selection of Spanish, French and domestic wines, as well as imported and domestic beers. The Morrows seem to enjoy the hard work that comes with this busy, well-loved place. Situated for a supreme view of Puget Sound, the balcony at the Copacabana is also a terrific perch to take in all the fascination of Pike Place Market.
Visa. Master charge.

Louie's Cuisine of China

5100 15TH AVE. N.W. JUST NORTH OF
BALLARD BRIDGE
782-8855

HOURS:
LUNCH: MONDAY-FRIDAY
11:30 A.M.-3:00 P.M.
DINNER: MONDAY-THURSDAY
3:00 P.M.-12:30 A.M.
FRIDAY 3:00 P.M.-1:30 A.M.
SATURDAY 4:00 P.M.-1:30 A.M.
SUNDAY 3:00 P.M.-11:00 P.M.
RESERVATIONS RECOMMENDED

Louie's Cuisine of China represents the third generation of Louie family restaurants in Seattle. It all began in 1905 with Charley Louie, a pioneer in Seattle's thriving Chinese restaurant business. He believed in using only the finest ingredients, preparing them expertly, and serving them with courtesy and style. This kind of integrity is amply evident in the latest Louie family restaurant located in Ballard. This restaurant is a remarkable achievement; an elegant blend of contemporary comfort and authentic cuisine. Dining in the Chinese manner is an art which involves combining different dishes that complement and contrast each other. Louie's offers a sophisticated variety of dishes for those who enjoy practicing this art. Special dinners and banquets for up to 50 may include dishes not listed on the menu and can be arranged with one of the Louies on a 48-hour advance notice. For the less adventurous, Louie's offers 5 different family-style dinners, each one featuring a good sampling. The service is excellent. Waiters are glad to inform you of special dishes not listed on the menu or give you advice about creating your own special dinner.
Visa. Master Charge. BankAmericard. American Express.

La Villa Real

409 WALL STREET
622-6320
HOURS:
LUNCH -
MONDAY-FRIDAY 11:30-2:30
DINNER -
MONDAY-SATURDAY 5:00-10:00
SUNDAY 5:00-9:00

La Villa Real, to put it quite simply, serves about the best Mexican food in Seattle. Fortunately, not many people know this yet, so if you catch a meal there now, you may get in ahead of the crowds. Tucked away on Wall Street, off 4th Avenue, brothers Jimmy and Gary Coury keep a regular clientele of old and new friends very well fed. These two former Los Angelinos of Syrian-Lebanese descent (yes, they really cook authentically Mexican) pride themselves on serving only the freshest food, expertly prepared so that it looks as good as it tastes. While the menu includes all the recognizable favorites, you are also advised to try one of the fine selections of unusual dishes, too. Cocktails, wine and very good Mexican beer are all available. The atmosphere is pleasant and informal, portions are generous, prices are reasonable, and the Courys are the most entertaining and congenial of hosts. Visa. Master Charge.

Matzoh Momma Delicatessen and Restaurant

**509 - 15TH EAST
324-MAMA
HOURS: MONDAY-SATURDAY
8:00 A.M.-11:00 P.M.
SUNDAY 8:00 A.M.-5:00 P.M.**

Now here's a restaurant even your mother would approve of. God forbid you should be eating in one of those awful fast food joints where you don't know what they put in the food, or an overpriced fancy schmancy place where the waiters treat you rotten and feed you sauces that could give you a heart attack or worse. But Matzoh Momma, now here's a different matter. This authentic Jewish deli-restaurant serves nothing but great food, made from old family recipes and the finest ingredients. Owners Pip and Miriam Myerson have assembled a good bunch of people who help them in a place that is more like home than anything else. The chicken soup with matzoh balls is just what the doctor ordered, not to mention the best bagels, lox and cream cheese this side of Brooklyn. You will also find the freshest homemade goods at Matzoh Momma, along with a friendly deli counter that allows you to eat it there or take it out. Matzoh Momma will cater any occasion, and they will even pack you a tasty brown bag lunch with a cookie. Now, that's nice! Call Matzoh Momma for details. Matzoh Momma Delicatessen and Restaurant has has imported beer and wine, Dr. Brown's famous sodas for homesick East Coast types and a complete bar service is coming soon.

Red Robin
Burger & Spirits Emporium

**3272 FUHRMAN
CORNER OF EASTLAKE AVENUE E.
AT SOUTH END OF UNIVERSITY BRIDGE
323-0917
138 NORTHGATE PLAZA
AT NORTH END OF SHOPPING MALL
365-0933
PLEASE CALL FOR INFORMATION
ON HOURS OF BUSINESS.**

If you've spent any time at the University of Washington, then you know about the Red Robin. It's a Husky hang-out that goes back 40 years. But ever since it was taken over by Seattle restaurateur Gerry Kingen and turned into the Red Robin Burger & Spirits Emporium, it has become a city-wide attraction. The original Red Robin still counts the college crowd among its loyal dining and drinking patrons, but everyone likes its casual, natural wood interior and deck overlooking Portage Bay. The Red Robin at Northgate has its own variations in decor, notably an elegant hand-carved rosewood antique bar. This location has more of a family atmosphere; there's even an electronic games room to encourage kids to let the old folks dine in peace for a change. The menu is the same in both places . . . an entertaining, tongue-in-cheek salute to the burger in all its manifestations. Purists can opt for the tried-and-true cheeseburger, leaving the more esoteric Bonsai Burger, Godfather, Turbulent Tummy and El Taco Burger to the non-conformists. The Red Robin also offers a good choice of steaks, salads, soups, fish & chips, and lots of desserts. The drink menu is as big as the food menu, with loads of amusingly-named house specials that will curl your hair. This restaurant idea has gone over so well with Seattle people that two new Red Robins are opening soon, downtown and on Capitol Hill.
Visa. Master Charge.

City Picnics

117 S. MAIN STREET
682-2067
410 SPRING STREET
682-8183
HOURS: MONDAY-FRIDAY 7:00-8:00
SATURDAY 9:00-8:00
SUNDAY 10:00-6:00

City Picnics has a style all its own: fast food with a lot of class. They are two cafeteria-style restaurants, one in Pioneer Square and one downtown, that both provide quick service in a lovely, relaxed setting. All the food is freshly made on the premises. The menu focuses on daily specials that can be anything from Seafood Struedel to Jambalaya. City Picnics does a lot of different things very well. Their bakers work around the clock to make sure there's always fresh brioche to go with your morning cup of Starbucks Viennese blend coffee. Lunchtime features lots of healthy gourmet sandwiches, hearty soups, crisp salads, and a special quiche every day. All in all, they create about 30 different soups and salads on a rotating basis. Desserts are very special . . . homemade pies, carrot cake, puddings. And if there are gooier, softer, nuttier cinnamon rolls around we certainly haven't heard about it. Richard and Donna Turner seem to know what people want in a city eatery. You can dine in to classical music, candlelight and wine. But they'll also cater, deliver or pack it up and send you off on a proper city picnic.

Visa. Master Charge.

For Women

Photo: Historical Society of Seattle & King County

Rhododendron time in Seattle is fairly spectacular, only I can't think when rhododendrons are in bloom.

E.B. White, ''Letters''

Photo: Marsha Burns

Silver Lining

607 2ND AVENUE
622-0197
HOURS: TUESDAY-SATURDAY 11:00-6:00
PLEASE CALL FOR AN APPOINTMENT.

The Silver Lining is a small shop specializing in custom-designed and created women's fashions. From its beginnings in the space once used by a tailor, the Silver Lining has grown by reputation and word-of-mouth to be one of Seattle's leading sources of unique custom clothing. Tucked far away from retail giants to the north, the Silver Lining nestles behind a massive stone arch in an interesting space that was once the entrance to the Butler Hotel. The salon itself is a statement of quiet elegance, a perfect setting to view and discuss exquisite couture garments. Although the business is only 5 years old, owner Karen Bell has been a student of fashion for nearly 20 years. Her training includes 13 years at the Children's Creative Art School of the Music & Art Foundation and 3 years at the Rudolph Schaeffer School of Design in San Francisco. She started out at the age of 5 sketching and creating her designs in miniature, guided by her mother, a sewing expert and teacher. Couture construction, high fashion awareness, timeless style and strict attention to detail are the elements that make each Silver Lining creation a highly individualized fashion statement.
Master Charge.

Nelly Stallion

1311 N.E. 45TH STREET
633-3950
HOURS: MONDAY-
SATURDAY 10:00-6:00

The reason Nelly Stallion always has exclusive designer pieces you can't find anywhere else is because owner Michael Spiegel virtually commutes to New York, England and the continent, in search of unique and beautiful clothing. What amazes is that he's maintained this energetic pace throughout the ten years since he opened Nelly Stallion. The looks Michael finds are varied . . . updated casual sportswear in the newest, brightest colors; low-key traditional styles in natural hues; and extravagant fantasies for memorable evenings. Nelly Stallion was out in front of the natural fabrics trend, encouraging women to appreciate the pleasing textures of silk, linen, wool and cotton. The collection of contemporary clothing here is perenially one of the richest in Seattle. There is a wide price range, from extremely reasonable all the way up to the unabashedly-expensive-and-worth-it. Everything from shoes to shirts, pants, dresses, and bold handknit sweaters are chosen to impart that distinctive, even avant-garde, high fashion impression.
Visa. Master Charge. American Express.

Dita Boutique

603 BROADWAY AVENUE E.
329-2777
HOURS: SUNDAY 12:00-5:00
MONDAY-THURSDAY 10:30-6:30
FRIDAY 10:30-8:30
SATURDAY 10:30-6:30
BY APPOINTMENT AFTER STORE HOURS.

Dita Boutique is that shop on Capitol Hill that has those wonderfully imaginative, traffic-stopping window displays. But this place would be on every Seattle woman's list of favorite shops anyway, because the clothing selection is as irresistable as the presentation. You'll find the latest designer collections from the fashion capitals of the world . . . wool blazers by Paul Stanley, silk dresses by Ceil Hughes, wool dresses by joanie char, blouses from Insight and Regina Porter, sweaters by Cygne, I.B. Diffusions and SW1, as well as a large selection of designer jeans and pants by Calvin Klein, Gloria Vanderbilt and others. Dita showcases the contemporary, the casual, and the cosmopolitan; looks in quality separates that give you the confidence of a total effect with lots of stimulating variety. The shop is widely used by busy professional women who need good-looking pieces in current styles that can tolerate an active career and travel schedule. Dita Boutique is also a good bet when you're after a striking one-of-a-kind article . . . those real gems that add a spark of individuality to your wardrobe.
Visa. Master Charge.

Lady Albert Ltd.

1335 FIFTH AVENUE
RAINIER SQUARE
622-3970
HOURS: MONDAY-SATURDAY 10:00-6:00

Lady Albert Ltd., a leading Seattle women's shop, is best known for classic sportswear in natural fabrics and colors — the kind of clothes that seem to get better the longer you own them. LAL offers a carefully edited collection of the best traditional styles from New York, the British Isles and Europe including coats and suits from Dorene of Dublin; Scottish lambswool, Shetland and cashmere sweaters; Austin Hill sportswear; Burberry's raincoats; tartan skirts by Aljean of Canada; Liberty of London scarves as well as tailored shirts, skirts, dresses and blazers. The selection of all-cotton shirts and blouses is particularly impressive, with solids, plaids and prints plus classic Oxford button-downs. Perhaps more than anything else, Lady Albert is the final word in Seattle for women's sweaters . . . they've cornered every possible color, style and weight, from bulky Welsh handknits to the finest cashmeres. At LAL you will find clothing conveniently arranged by size in an atmosphere made warm and comfortable by Oriental rugs and greenery. The service by the friendly staff at LAL is always available to assist customers in creating a timeless wardrobe from this fine selection of classics. Alterations are available, along with a monogramming service on the premises to add interest and individuality to your purchases.
Visa. Master Charge. American Express. Lay-away Plans.

 **Puella**

**1333 5TH AVENUE
RAINIER SQUARE
682-2638
HOURS: MONDAY-SATURDAY 9:30-6:00**

Puella has a rather special approach to fashion. It was created by Lydia Williams to serve the needs of the sophisticated working woman. The shop is both beautiful and comfortable, with a charming sitting corner where you can relax amid Victoria furnishings and glance through the latest fashion magazines. Customers are encouraged to bring along items from their own wardrobe and take time to match them with new purchases. Advice on planning a career wardrobe is happily offered. Lydia does her buying in New York and concentrates on finding rising young designers whose prices are reasonable. The emphasis is on easy-care, quality-made separates with classic lines for maximum versatility, but the selection also includes imaginative, unique pieces, in everything from dresses to accessories. Puella is the kind of place where you can make one stop and plan an entire season's wardrobe in an afternoon, and for a busy working woman, there's no better service around.

Visa. Master Charge. American Express.

Sbocco

**100 MERCER STREET
(HANSEN BAKING CO.)
285-2140
HOURS: MONDAY-
SATURDAY 10:00-6:00
FRIDAY UNTIL 8:00
SUNDAY 12:00-5:00**

**528 UNION (CORNER
OF 6TH & UNION)
624-9900
HOURS: MONDAY-
SATURDAY 10:00-6:00**

**602 BELLEVUE WAY N.E.
(EASTSIDE)
455-9930
HOURS: MONDAY-
SATURDAY 10:00-6:00**

Sbocco is a Seattle fashion success story. This shop began 5 years ago as a tiny, exclusive designer boutique in the Hansen Baking Company complex. It created such a demand for quality fashion that there are now two more locations, in downtown Seattle and Bellevue. The name comes from the Italian word meaning "outlet" and that's exactly what Sbocco is. It's a source of sophisticated clothing with European styling. The looks vary widely, from the outrageously avant-garde to the ultra feminine and the classically simple. But whatever the look, quality is never sacrificed.

Sbocco features the best of the established status designers and new young fashion innovators. The focus is on natural fibers, but the shop is always on watch for imaginative use of fabric blends. Sbocco's salespeople keep abreast of pieces reflecting the latest trends as well as the dependable basics and can give you advice on how to achieve the best of both worlds. Some of Seattle's best known television personalities and business women avail themselves of this service. Sbocco is a boon to any woman who wants to dress for success.
Visa. Master Charge. American Express.

Apogee/Perigee

4224 E. MADISON
4227 E. MADISON
325-2848
HOURS: MONDAY-SATURDAY
11:00 AM-6:30 PM

Here is the smart way to shop, away from the maddening crowd in beautiful Madison Park where the Lake Washington scape has imposed a welcomely relaxed pace to commerce in the community, and where a parking spot is at least possible. This is where you'll find two of the best fashion resources in town . . . Apogee, one of Seattle's first boutiques, and its counterpoint Perigee, a store dedicated to traditional women's clothing. Apogee carries the latest news in fashion . . . design jeans by Sasoon, Cacharel, Gloria Vanderbilt and Calvin Klein. They also feature Pierre D'Alby and Daniel Hechter. Across the street, the mood at Perigee is classic and timeless . . . but never dull. Updated colors, tweeds and special hand-knits suggest complementary accents to the ample selection of suits with pants or skirts, the most important basics of every woman's wardrobe. This focus shows up in lines like J.G. Hook, John Meyer, Dalton and Harvé Bernard. They've also added a romantic note with lingerie . . . notably, gowns and robes. Apogee takes pride in its small-size specialty, while Perigee carries a full range up to and including size 14. They're both open until 6:30 p.m. so there's time to get there after work and browse, even if you don't live in Madison Park.
Visa. Master Charge.

L.W. Schrader

832 102ND AVENUE N.E.
BELLEVUE
455-0883
HOURS: MONDAY-SATURDAY 10:00-6:00

When you're shopping for clothes, very seldom do you see something on the rack, fall in love with it, try it on, it's perfect and you're happy. Lynwood Schrader knows that for most women it takes time and attention to find the right addition to a wardrobe. L.W. Schrader is in a little brown house just north of Bellevue Square. It's cozy and leisurely. You can even sit next to the fireplace and have a cup of tea...but when you're trying on clothes, you get the kind of attention that you'd only expect at an exclusive designers' salon. Quality is the common thread through the selection of understated contemporary clothing here. That means most of the suits, separates, dresses and accessories are made with natural fabrics...silk, wool, gabardine, wool tweed, linen...and the styles are contemporary, yet classical with the kind of traditional tailoring that never goes out of fashion. Some of the quality lines featured are trousers by Barry, pants by LePainty and Chris Allan, silk dresses by Jack Mulqueen and D.D. Dominick and other beautiful fashions by Pierre D'Alby and Norman Todd. We live in a climate where it is not necessary to have distinctly separate winter and summer wardrobes, and so L.W. Schrader focuses on seasonless fashion. For added convenience and service L.W. Schrader has its own charge card and simple alterations are free.

Margaret Swan
Working Suits for Women

932-5007
PLEASE CALL FOR AN APPOINTMENT.

Margaret Swan is a designer/seamstress who has decided to specialize in something working women have been looking for . . . fine custom-tailored suits. She believes that career women deserve the same attention to fit and longevity that men have always expected from their business clothing. Margaret will create entire wardrobes of coordinated pieces including jackets, skirts, pants and vests to provide a range of easy work-day decisions. Her designs may be adjusted to accommodate the needs of each individual, and her excellent sewing techniques and workmanship assure a perfect fit. Her pieces feature full lining, ample, usable pockets, and exquisite detailing. The price for a suit runs about $250 to $300 depending upon the chosen fabric and design. Her training and experience are top-notch, but above all, she is a women's tailor who has focused on something women really need. Margaret enjoys her work, and regards each piece as finished only when her client is completely happy with the result.

Totally Michael's

1333 - 5TH AVENUE
RAINIER SQUARE
622-4920
HOURS: MONDAY-
SATURDAY 10:00-6:00

Totally Michael's is a byword among Seattle trend-setters. The boutique made history in 1971 when it became the first downtown specialty store catering to the needs of working women. The owners, Mses. Michael Smith and Carol Baldwin, have an unerring eye for superb tailoring. Their collection of contemporary fashions places an accent on domestic and imported ready-to-wear, with a special emphasis on natural fibres such as wool, silk and cotton. The labels include the who's who of fashion . . . Stanley Blacker, Pierre D'Alby, Chris Allan, La Belle France, Adolfo, and Paul Stanley. Michael's middle to upper-end prices reflect the shop's commitment to quality. Blazers range from $110 to $300; suits from $150 to $400. The real fashion finds here are the excellent values on sweaters, $22 to $70 and dresses, $50 to $120; all available in sizes from 4-14.
Visa. Master Charge.

The Satin Goose

519 UNION STREET
682-6014
HOURS: MONDAY-SATURDAY 10:00-6:00

The Satin Goose is a clothing store for women of all ages. The emphasis is on good quality, versatile separates that don't need to break the bank to work well in your wardrobe. There are jackets, blouses, skirts, and pants that fit . . . colorful and substantial pieces which can be combined in any number of ways to create looks for practically every activity. You don't need to wade through racks and racks of clothes to find what you want either. The sales people are willing to give full attention to individual tastes, and will direct you to selections that complement your figure and personal image. There are clothes for work and play and after-five, along with a fascinating array of accessories . . . unusual jewelry designs, belts and scarves, and some especially beautiful designer hats from New York. The prevailing attitude at The Satin Goose is that each woman probably already knows the look that suits her best, so you won't be intimidated into buying the most avant-garde designs in the store, but rather encouraged to express yourself in comfortable choices. One of the nicest lines at The Satin Goose is a collection of one-of-a-kind handwoven separates, created by an Oregon artist, which may be just the thing to make sure no-one else at the dinner party is wearing the same thing. Visa. Master Charge. American Express.

Nubia's

4116 E. MADISON AVENUE
325-4354
HOURS: MONDAY-SATURDAY 10:30-6:00

Nubia Penuela-Ryan of Colombia has introduced to Seattle an ethnic fashion elegance unmatched anywhere else in town, by featuring rare collections from all over the world at her Madison Park Shop. At Nubia's, fine imported clothes with a flair and a contemporary touch are delightful reminders that we all like to be a little bit different. Nubia has an eye for selecting that combines "different" and "tasteful" in a way that elicits compliments and curiosity . . . "where did you get that?" Although most of the garments are from Latin America, she is in touch with buyers all over the world. The clothes are usually handmade in natural fibers that make them especially suited to the Northwest climate . . . and those bright, true colors give a welcome lift on a gloomy day. You'll find dresses, jackets, skirts, capes, scarves, jewelry and accessories of all kinds. The hand-knit woolens from South America are particularly beautiful. Shopping at Nubia's is the most fun when Nubia herself is there. This charming lady will regale you with fun conversation, show you the latest arrivals, and help you make the very best selections.

Unicorn Textiles

1333 - 5TH AVENUE
RAINIER SQUARE
292-9941
HOURS: MONDAY-SATURDAY 9:30-6:00

Unicorn Textiles specializes in sophisticated fabrics for people with urban tastes and a desire to create quality high-fashion wardrobes on their own. The store is beautifully laid out, showcasing one of the finest fabric selections you'll find anywhere in the city. The majority of the fabrics are natural fibers — wool, silk, linen and cotton — from the best domestic and European mills, but the Unicorn also stocks a wide variety of quality blends, both prints and vibrant colors in every weight and weave imaginable. There are nubby, textured wools and fine melton weaves, Harris tweeds from England and the newest woolen goods from France and Italy. The silk comes from all over the world, Europe as well as India and the Orient, and the silky polyesters will please even the most discriminating eye. You'll find cotton from England, Italy and Switzerland. The pattern service includes Vogue and Folkwear patterns, and the shop also provides tailoring and dressmaking services. A special touch at Unicorn Textiles is the attractive boutique corner with an assortment of one-of-a-kind textile gifts and whimsical soft sculptures . . . many with the graceful unicorn motif.
Visa. Master Charge.

The Silk Thread

**616 BROADWAY AVENUE E.
323-6955
HOURS: MONDAY-
FRIDAY 10:00-8:00
SATURDAY 10:00-6:00**

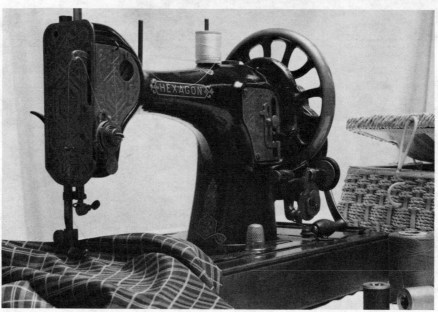

The Silk Thread is a top-quality sewing store on Capitol Hill specializing in beautiful designer fabrics, and all the expert services that go into transforming them into beautiful clothing. Owners Cheryl Arrants and Jan Asbjornsen keep in close touch with sources in New York to obtain the same fabrics used by internationally known designers like Calvin Klein, Ralph Lauren, Scott Barrie and Anne Klein. You can create these fashions for yourself at a tremendous saving, using the Vogue Designer Patterns available at The Silk Thread. Or, if you prefer, they will refer you to one of the many talented seamstresses and designers in Seattle, who've helped many women get the benefit of designer clothing with a perfect custom fit. The shop is geared to the needs of busy working women, many of whom regard The Silk Thread's wardrobe planning service as the basis for successful career clothing. Cheryl and Jan make efforts to help customers do careful selecting . . . they keep the shop open until 8 p.m. on weekdays to allow the luxury of unhurried decisions; there's a full-length 3-way mirror with different light settings so you'll see how a fabric really looks on you . . . and a terrific Vogue Designer Pattern exchange system. The Silk Thread is a place where young Seattle designers go to find the same fabrics and sewing accessories used in the production of nationally known labels. In fact, The Silk Thread is a sort of community center for women who equate quality, individually-created fashion with money in the bank.
Visa. Master Charge.

Body Faire

4219½ UNIVERSITY WAY N.E.
632-8626
HOURS: MONDAY-
SATURDAY 10:00-5:30
THURSDAY UNTIL 9:00

Body Faire is one of those seductive little shops that are impossible to pass by. You think you might pop in and out in five minutes, but a half-hour and one shelf later, you're still there, wondering how such a small space could hold so many wonderful things. The selection isn't huge; it's just that everything is special and rare and perfect for someone you know, especially yourself. True to its name, Body Faire carries its own line of natural-based personal care products for pampering every pore: shampoo, massage oil, lotions, soaps, creams and bubble bath. There are also all kinds of other treasures, hand-picked by owners Sherry Howard and Mary Robison, that never fail to captivate even the most sophisticated shopper. The stock is always changing, but usually includes such things as designer earrings, lacquer boxes, Chinese purses, wallets, baskets and umbrellas, natural fabric clothing, wool hats, outrageous socks, note cards, ceramic mugs and silly toothbrushes. The best part about all this is the reasonable price range; that, combined with the consistent quality, makes Body Faire an indulgence you can well afford.
Visa. Master Charge.

Susan Barry

1318 FIFTH AVENUE
625-9200
HOURS: MONDAY-SATURDAY 10:00-6:00

The beautiful lingerie at Susan Barry would make any woman feel pampered and extravagant. There's simply nothing better than sleeping in 100% cotton or silk hand-embroidered nightgowns, and the remarkable selection at this brand new store is a dream come true. You'll find designer lingerie, sleepwear and loungewear to satisfy all your cravings for luxury here. Everything at Susan Barry is chosen for extra touches that please . . . embroidery, imported lace, exquisite delicacy. The displays are beautiful and imaginative; you can almost take in the entire stock in one sweeping glance. Sizes range from petite to large and the price range is moderate to expensive, but the quality and workmanship on the fashions here make them well worth the cost. Susan Barry has a seamstress on call for alterations to ensure a perfect fit.
Visa. Master Charge. American Express.

Nail Me

DOWNTOWN
682-8226

EAST BELLEVUE
747-4400

BELLEVUE
453-8226

RENTON
226-6030

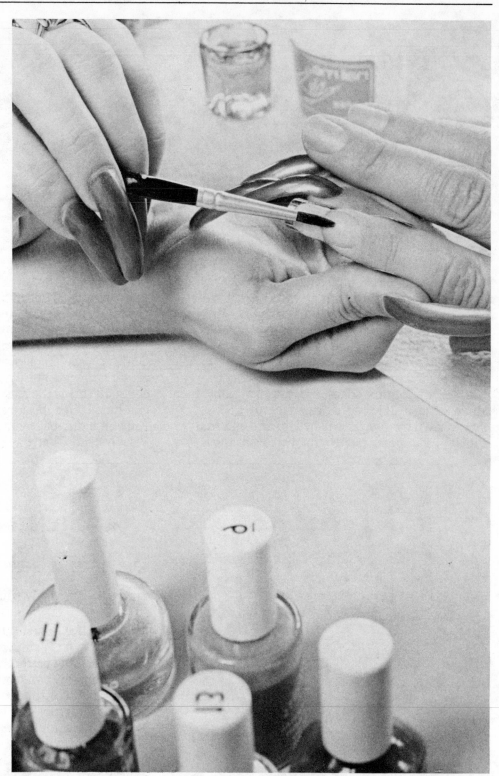

Nail Me is one of those terrific services that make it all worthwhile. There's something about long, polished nails that makes you feel completely cared for and just plain pampered. At Nail Me, you can get long nails even if you're one of those women who can't stop biting her own. Kate Wright is the owner and she knows about nails. Long-lasting and impossible to tell from the real thing, her product is actually sculpted right over your own nails and can be made any length you choose. Those lucky few who can grow their own perfect ten can get nail strengthening treatments, nail wraps and repairs for broken nails. A licensed cosmetologist, Kate also manufactures her own line of fine nail products, employs her own chemists and researchers, and will consult with you on any nail problem. If someone you know bites her nails, may we suggest a gift certificate from Nail Me? It might just be the most perfect, unusual and welcome gift you could dream up. And if you've never treated yourself to a manicure or pedicure before, try it at Nail Me. You'll wonder why you waited so long to cultivate such a pleasant habit.

For Men

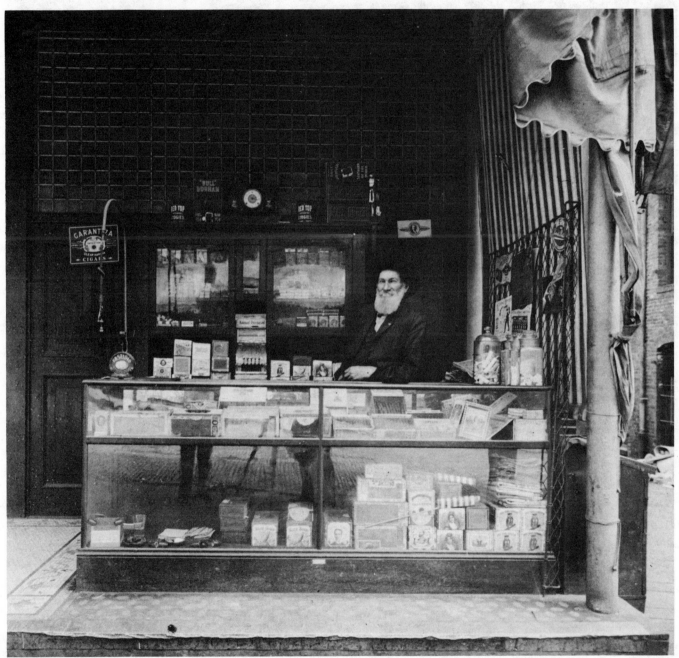

Photo: Historical Society of Seattle & King County

In the late summer of 1966, Carol and I arrived in Seattle, set out at once to walk its hills and shores and to explore into the mountain ranges scarped along the entire horizons east and west of the city. We were on new ground of the continent, and stretched gratefully to it.

Ivan Doig, ''This House of Sky''

Albert Limited

1210 - 4TH AVENUE
623-3970
HOURS: MONDAY-SATURDAY 9:00-5:30

As you walk into Albert Limited, you are greeted with a sense of warmth and tradition established over forty years. All the important accoutrements are there: inviting Shepard's Market Square windows, Tudor architecture, pegged oak floors, antiques and Oriental rugs. They provide a handsome background for the soft shoulder clothing, furnishings and sportswear displayed. The natural soft shoulder design, like classic architecture, will long endure fleeting fashions. Albert Limited emphasizes rigorous standards of design and merchandise by using only the most select fabrics from England, Scotland and the United States. Present owner Richard Brown and founder Harold Hoak (a recognized pioneer in natural shoulder clothing) insist on the finest clothing and accessories. Albert Limited is the exclusive Pacific Northwest representative for Southwick suits, featuring the traditional three-button St. Andrews and the slimmer, updated two-button Sterling models. Accessories like Alan Paine sweaters, Invertere outerwear, Sero shirts and Talbott neckwear reflect their standards. Men who agree with this philosophy find that classic taste at Albert Limited is never out of fashion.
Visa. Master Charge. American Express.

 # Michael's Bespoke Tailors

407 UNION ST.,
RAINIER SQUARE ON UNION
623-4785
HOURS: MONDAY-FRIDAY 9:30-6:00
SATURDAY 9:30-5:00
OR BY APPOINTMENT

For three years in a row, Esquire has named Michael's Bespoke Tailors one of the ten best design tailors in the country. This is not surprising, since owner Michael Weinstein's grandfather was a leading city tailor for many years, and Michael carries on that tradition in grand manner. To men for whom fit and fashion are all, this is the place to come for a perfectly cut, personally fitted wardrobe. Michael's fashion experts custom-design everything from shirts, jackets and trousers to full suits and overcoats. Each piece is made of the finest natural fibers in the world, imported from the mills of England, France and Italy. Michael's can design an overcoat or suit to specification, whether it's the very latest Italian look or something in the honored Seville Row tradition. Many men do business here because Michael's offers the convenience they require. The tailors keep accurate records of each customer's measurements and preferences on file. So, instead of spending time shopping, Michael's clients simply order what they need, confident that the fit and look will be exactly right.
Visa. Master Charge.

The Country Gentleman

**10116 N.E. 8TH AVENUE
BELLEVUE
455-2969
HOURS: MONDAY BY APPOINTMENT
TUESDAY-FRIDAY 10:00-8:00
SATURDAY 10:00-5:30**

Traditional, but contemporary, is the theme at The Country Gentleman. They've taken the best qualities of clothing from the past . . . elegance, fine tailoring and natural fabrics . . . and applied them to the needs and fashion consciousness of the modern professional man. You can find the natural shoulder look here, but also branch out into a more fitted, younger look. The Country Gentleman carries a full range of clothing and accessories, including suits, sport coats, shoes, sweaters, cotton underwear, and one of the largest selections of all-cotton sport and dress shirts in the city. Of course, they employ a master tailor to assure the impeccable fit that you demand. At The Country Gentleman, they keep an eye on the new while retaining all respect for the old.
Visa. Master Charge. BankAmericard. House Accounts.

Jeffrey Michael

**4TH AVENUE & UNION STREET
RAINIER SQUARE
625-9891
HOURS:
MONDAY-SATURDAY 9:30-6:00
AND BY APPOINTMENT**

Young professional men in Seattle who desire clothing that is both fashionable and elegant, usually find it at Jeffrey Michael. Buyer/manager Mike Sophie attempts, in his travels, to find the latest looks in the very best quality fabrics and tailoring, while keeping an eye on the price tag. The collection at Jeffrey Michael is accordingly in good taste, but never stuffy or stodgey. Customers from all over the country shop here because the selection is so distinctive and imparts a definite fashion-conscious look to a man's wardrobe. Sports coats and suits by Sergio Valentino are part of that look, along with contemporary woolen sweaters by Sabre of Great Britain. Dedicated to total fashion,

Jeffrey Michael has an exceptional selection of shoes featuring the styles of Bruno Magli, French Shriner and Cole-haan. Gift shopping for men is no problem here. You'll find solid silver key chains with enamel inlays, sterling "doubling cubes" with turquoise inlaid numbers, ice buckets with personality, and many other unusual, but tasteful items from all over the world. Jeffrey Michael assures the most expert, personalized service and for custom made suits, shirts, or jackets, their full-time tailor has impeccable credentials.
Visa. Master Charge. American Express. Diners Club. Carte Blanche.

Jeffrey Jensen

**WINSLOW MALL,
WINSLOW, WASHINGTON
842-6400
HOURS: MONDAY-
SATURDAY 10:00-6:00**

For years, Seattle's city dwellers have boarded ferries to Bainbridge Island in search of beautiful scenery, clean expanses of waterfront, and pastoral calm. It's only since Jeffrey Jensen clothing store opened in Winslow that people have been making the trip to find the latest fashions. And why not? This shop for men and women focuses on imaginative and high-quality clothing. It's really a delight to shop where the salespeople invite you to enjoy a cup of coffee while you discuss your wardrobe needs and design a look to suit your lifestyle. Jeffrey Jensen is more like a full service fashion salon than a clothing store. The collection is predominantly for men, but the women's line includes beautiful 3-piece suits, suede jeans, pleated pants, and hand-painted silk dresses. The emphasis is on natural fibers in both men's and women's wear, featuring wool blasers, raw silk pants, leather jackets and unusual items like rabbit hair blend shirts and sweatshirts in mink. The men's look focuses on casual elegance ... Saturday clothes with enough panache to carry a well-dressed man through the week. Jeffrey Jensen is unpretentious, yet distinctive, and fast becoming one of the best reasons to visit Bainbridge Island.

For Men & Women

Photo: Historical Society of Seattle & King County

When the world comes to an end, Seattle will still have one year to go.

Dick Vertlieb

Design Products Clothing

**208 1ST AVENUE S.
624-7795
HOURS: MONDAY-
SATURDAY
11:00 AM-5:30 PM**

Design Products Clothing is one of the most attractive stores in Pioneer Square. The reasons for that may not be instantly obvious, because it is an intentionally uncluttered place; spacious and welcomely free of all decor contrivances. It strikes an attitude more than an ''atmosphere'' and makes for very pleasant shopping. Vicki Tsuchida is the owner, and the shop's success is a reflection of her approach to clothing. Her genuine manner and enthusiasm for good design have become rather widely appreciated by people who work and shop in the area. The selection centers on simply designed suits and separates of good quality and rich texture. The stock is by no means large, but it doesn't have to be because Vicki's taste is terrific. She tries to choose affordable things that look good on just about everyone and carries a good range of colors and sizes when she find things she knows her customers will like. The clothes here are the kind that bridge the gap for people who enjoy being well turned out but prefer a casual look. Some of the lines you'll find are Cacharel for men and women, Moda Fiorentini and Pierre D'Alby, who make clothes you feel good about buying because you know you won't get tired of them. There is also a fine selection of accessories, some of them custom-made for the store. And if you find that a perfect fit off the rack a little elusive, you might enquire about the skirt and pants patterns offered by Design Products Clothing's custom sewing service.

Visa. Master Charge.

Courrèges

1518 6TH AVENUE
682-7554
HOURS: MONDAY-FRIDAY 10:00-6:00
SATURDAY 10:00-5:00

Virtually every haute couture designer in the world now manufactures a ready-to-wear line, but few people remember that it was Andre Courrèges who inaugurated this trend with his startling geometric dresses, now regarded as quintessential Sixties fashion. Fifteen years and many newsworthy creations and clients later, Courrèges designs are still synonymous with the best in European fashion. There are now Courrèges stores in the world's most important places . . . here since 1975, when Georgia Schorr opened her store and made the famous French designer's line available in Seattle. The clothes are exciting. Both the men's and the women's lines bear the impeccable workmanship and quality fabrics for which Courrèges is noted. The women's evening wear is bright, delicate, feminine, but unfettered . . . suits and coordinating daywear are elegantly simple and very dressy. Everything is custom-hemmed and anything may be altered. There is also a selection of accessories for all seasons and occasions, including the Courrèges signature fragrance. For investment-quality couturier fashion, the Courrèges approach is unsurpassed.

Visa. Master Charge. American Express. Diners Club. House Accounts.

The Village Trader

915 BELLEVUE WAY N.E.
BELLEVUE
454-4531
HOURS: MONDAY-
FRIDAY 10:00-8:00
SATURDAY 10:00-6:00
SUNDAY 12:00-5:00

The Village Trader clothing store in Bellevue believes in tradition from the ground up. That's why their shop is designed to feel like a New England country store . . . with paned windows, planked wood floors, wood and brass fixtures, and antique furnishings. The clothes they carry reflect the same dedication to quality. Owners Bob and Chris Nelson regard clothes as virtual lifetime investments and feel they should be chosen accordingly. The selection focuses unequivocally on classic designs for men and women. Suits, separates, shirts, sweaters, pants, skirts and accessories are the components of a traditional look that has proven consistently fashionable for several decades; pieces that need only minor modifications to stay current. The collection centers on natural fabrics, from real Harris Tweeds to wool flannel, corduroy, camel hair cashmeres and 100% cotton. These are clothes that fit any lifestyle and move from work to evening to the country with aplomb and style.
Visa. Master Charge.

Roots Footwear

4519 UNIVERSITY WAY N.E.
634-2382
HOURS: MONDAY-SATURDAY 10:00-6:00

Roots was founded on the premise that fashion and comfort in footwear need not be a contradiction in terms. Once identified as the negative heel company, Roots has since gone on to become a design success in regularly-heeled footwear to complement a fashion statement that fits Seattle's lifestyle. It's a naturally casual but tailored look that calls for the new Roots "Classics" . . . Wingtips, Jazz Oxfords and Spectators; all variations on stylish versatility, and all bearing the characteristic Roots comfort. There's also an exciting collection of Roots boots for every fashion persuasion, fine-leather designed for longevity, support and easy motion. A limited quantity are handcrafted from a soon-to-be-vintage suede. Roots has its own line of leather everyday handbags, and features a colorful array of natural fibre socks. Dedicated to simultaneous fashion and comfort, the people at Roots are proud to acknowledge that they've come up in the world, but their feet are still on the ground.

Visa. Master Charge.

Biagio

1312 - 4TH AVENUE
RAINIER SQUARE
623-3842
HOURS: MONDAY-SATURDAY 9:30-6:00

Leather and gold . . . that's Biagio. Even globe-trotting shoppers would agree that shops don't get more specialized than this. The dedication to these perfect mates makes the selection of fashion accessories at Biagio classic. You can find a fine leather valise that is smashing on its own, but you might be tempted to buy a 14K bracelet to go with it. The jewelery designs are chosen for clean cut lines which always look right. Biagio carries rings, stick pins, pierced earrings, charms, pendants, as well as chains, chains and more chains, all 14-karat precious. The fine leather collection displays the mark of many fine designers — Pierre Cardin, Etienne Aigner, Enny, Coach, Michael Scott, Aris, and Hartman. Biagio has wallets for men and women, checkbook covers, even passport folders, and because leather travels so well, the luggage selection specializes in ''carry-on'' items and garment bags. Leather gloves, hand bags, jewel boxes . . . the only things that aren't leather at Biagio are 14-karat.
Visa. Master Charge. American Express.

 Caswell-Massey of Seattle

1316 4TH AVENUE
RAINIER SQUARE
292-9483
HOURS: MONDAY-SATURDAY 9:30-5:30

Caswell-Massey is the oldest drugstore and perfumer in America. In fact, this establishment started in 1752, making it older than America itself. They still carry their famous No. 6 Cologne, created especially for George Washington. Anyone who's been to their wonderful old shop on Lexington Avenue in New York will appreciate how well Caswell-Massey in Seattle has captured the atmosphere and aroma of the original. The walls of this lovely shop are lined with wicker baskets and old wood and glass cabinets displaying the complete Caswell-Massey line. If you're a Caswell-Massey fan, then no-one need explain the line to you, and if you're not, well nothing short of a visit will do it justice. In 227 years of doing business all over the world, Caswell-Massey has gathered a remarkable collection of soaps, oils, fragrances and personal care products of all kinds; from the exotic to the practical, the elegant and the esoteric, from goose quill toothpicks to French crystal atomizers and much more. There are brand names here you won't find anywhere else. Pay a visit to Caswell-Massey and see it all for yourself.
Visa. Master Charge. American Express.

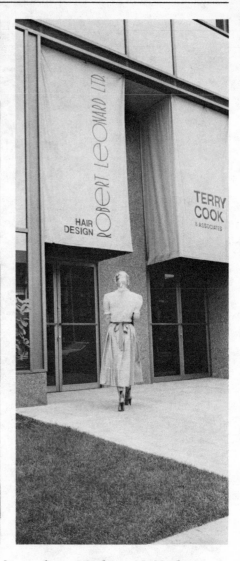

Robert Leonard

2033 SIXTH AVENUE
UNITED AIRLINES BUILDING
623-9666
HOURS: TUESDAY-SATURDAY 9:00-6:00

Ah, sweet calendar . . . red letter day and Robert Leonard. "Bop bop sho be do bo . . . Mama told me there'd be days like this, there'd be days like this, mama said (backup singers hit it) mama said, mama said." Y'know . . . I should . . . I should really send mother to Robert Leonard . . . she'd come out a completely new woman. "Mother, you don't need an analyst, you need a facialist." Remind me . . . I'm going to be late . . . 9:00 A.M.: Juliana, Esthetician for a Facial. Start right off with a fruit mask blended especially to my skin type. I'll skip breakfast . . . be faintly famished by lunch and order Escargots for a starter. Where are those sheer nylons?

. . . If I have a pedicure from Micki at 10:30 along with my manicure I can wear those open toed heels. My fingernails don't look too bad since Micki started paper wrapping them . . . but, I really should buy a new ring . . . something provocative around the stem of a wine glass. My jade comb . . . can't forget that! When Carolyn combs me out at 11:30, she can braid my pony tail and work in the jade comb . . . exotic . . . I'd like to look a bit exotic. Thank goodness for Dan, Dan, my make-up man at 12:00 . . . never fails me . . . gives me cheek bones . . . makes me feel so . . . so foreign. Pate . . . I'll start with pate instead. I don't really *like* snails, but it sounds so sophisticated to order them with the right accent . . . "Et pour vous, madame?" Slowly looking up from the menu with wide innocent eyes, no wrinkles thanks to Robert Leonard . . . "Mais, oui, les escargots s'il vous plait." I'm expected at Annique's at 12:45 . . . I'll have to ask Robert what time would be fashionably late . . . might take a bit of a promenade down Fifth first, window shopping. Umbrella! That's what I forgot!

Rosalie Cantrell & Associates

CORNER MARKET BUILDING, 2ND FLOOR
PIKE PLACE MARKET, 1ST & PIKE STREET
623-3430
HOURS: TUESDAY-SATURDAY 9:00-5:00

UNIVERSITY DISTRICT
1408 N.E. 43RD STREET
634-3940
HOURS: MONDAY-SATURDAY 9:00-5:00
EXCEPT THURSDAY 11:00-7:00

Rosalie Cantrell is a respected name in the national and international fashion world. She not only runs two of the best full-service hair salons, but she's deeply involved in shaping the fashion scene in Seattle. She began her business with a shop in the University District, which became popular with students and professionals alike, seeking the very latest fashion looks with efficient, no-nonsense service. Some of the best hair stylists in Seattle perfected their techniques in this very shop. Rosalie Cantrell's newest outlet in the Pike Place Market is one of the few places in town that boasts haircuts with a view. Situated in a beautifully remodeled space with high ceilings and large paneled windows overlooking the market, it has become a place where members of Seattle's downtown professional set like to spend their lunch hours . . . enjoying the benefits of the newest haircuts, perms and coloring techniques while watching ferryboats laze across Elliott Bay. Rosalie Cantrell's administrative offices are here too, where she supervises her consulting and educational programs and produces some of Seattle's most talked about hair and fashion extravaganzas. Rosalie Cantrell's was recently named by Harper's Bazaar as one of the top salons in the nation. The hours are very convenient, the staff is young and friendly and the customer is treated with personal attention and style.
Visa. Master Charge.

J'Ambry
Experts in Wearables

SUITE 311
SIXTH & PINE BUILDING
624-8070
PLEASE CALL FOR AN APPOINTMENT.

J'Ambry offers an unusual and indispensible service to busy, fashion-conscious men and women, who don't want to spend a small fortune in time or money putting together the perfect wardrobe. It is a group of competent fashion consultants, headed by Jan McLaughlin, who will help you select and organize a closet full of clothes you can depend on to be ready for all occasions. J'Ambry services vary . . . you can choose a one-hour consultation that includes an analysis of colors most suited to you, an explanation of wardrobe building, and a discussion of appropriate styles for your body type. Or the service can be extended to include a visit to your home to review and revamp your existing wardrobe. And to that end they'll compile a complete shopping list. If you don't have time to shop, J'Ambry can do that too, bringing selections to your home or office for final approval. Group workshops may be organized as well, and J'Ambry consultants can arrange special series-workshops or speaking engagements for your group. Taking its name from the old English word for closet, this specialty fashion concept makes a lot of sense. You'll wonder why it never occurred to you that there's an alternative to staring with furrowed brow at a closet full of white elephants.

Gary Bocz for Hair

523 PINE STREET
624-9134
HOURS: TUESDAY-SATURDAY 8:00-6:00

Next season's newest styles are currently under construction right now at Gary Bocz for Hair. Your hair is probably your most important fashion accessory, and it reflects your look and lifestyle as much as the clothes you wear. The stylists at Gary Bocz for Hair aim for a versatility that allows this personal expression. They discover who you are and how you feel so that the two of you can come up with the look most suited to your personality. The advice these talented people offer comes hand in hand with emphatic respect for the individual's wishes — they won't impose their ideas on you. Now, on the other hand, if you want to feel brand new or do something rare for an evening's fantasy, just sit back and know they'll create something wonderful. All Gary Bocz stylists keep in step with the latest techniques. It's a full-service salon; providing complete hair care and more . . . manicures, pedicures, as well as general fashion and make-up counselling. They work closely with J'Ambry on fashion consultation and Face Clinique on skin care and make-up, to create a total look personally developed for each client.
Visa. Master Charge.

Man in the Moon

**2621 - 5TH AVENUE
623-6330
HOURS: SEVEN DAYS
A WEEK 12-6:00
WATCH FOR NEW
CAPITOL HILL
LOCATION.**

Photo: Jeff Berger

Vintage clothing stores are very popular in Seattle, and amongst a number of good ones, Man in the Moon is top-of-the-line. You could even say it's the Cadillac of the field because owner Michael Berg has his own 1953 model to prove it. Both he and partner Janell de Varona are dedicated fans of Forties fashion and usually dress the part. Their store has an atmosphere to match, complete with jukebox, hat boxes, deco fixtures and those big comfy chairs we all wish they still made. The stock covers every decade since the Thirties, and includes jewelry and accessories from every period. Amongst much else, you'll find men's suits, furs, women's silk lingerie, and always a lovely collection of original dresses. Everything is in mint condition and ready to wear. It's a lot of fun to shop here but it also makes a lot of sense. The vintage look has been such a hit that reproductions abound. What they can't do is imitate the kind of quality that lasts for five decades. Why not go to the source? Man in the Moon offers a fashion identity that's always original.
Visa. Master Charge.

Northwest Fashion Institute

2028 FIFTH AVENUE
292-9282
HOURS: MONDAY-FRIDAY 9:00-6:00

Not everyone is born with a sense of presentation — the art of knowing what impression is made by a particular mode of dress or style of entrance. That's why there are professionals at the Northwest Fashion Institute whose pupose is to provide guidance in developing a well rounded, day-to-day sense of self. After a year of research and organization, the Institute has evolved into a facility offering seminars and programs related to personal image. These programs combine a mental and physical approach for men and women to define, develop, and project a personal style aimed at moving more confidently and successfully through both professional and social environments. Seminars include visual projection, mind and body maintenance, non-verbal and verbal communications. There are no resident instructors at the Northwest Fashion Institute. All the seminars and classes are taught by professionals who are experts in their fields. Director Pennie M. Pickering leads this progressive approach to help men and women fit their ever-changing roles, and do it with the kind of polish and presentation that has been important socially and professionally in every age of time.

Tina Peterson's Body Express

205 UNIVERSITY STREET
623-0702
CLASSES ARE SCHEDULED SEVEN DAYS A WEEK
6:30 A.M.-9:30 P.M.

Tina Peterson's Body Express is one of those rare places that get nothing but rave reviews from everybody who goes there. The first thing clients always mention is what a beautiful space this is. Those who expect the usual subterranean clammy basement gym are pleasantly surprised by the open, warm, second-storey space that looks like everybody's fantasy of a ballet rehearsal studio. Live music on guitar, piano and congas set the tempo. In such a wonderful environment, keeping in shape becomes a pleasure, not a chore. Classes are challenging and provide a real work-out, but they are taught with flair and imagination; they're enjoyable as well as beneficial. Tina Peterson has years of professional teaching and performing experience in ballet and body conditioning. Her skilled staff members offer classes for everyone from beginners to professional dancers who are interested in maintaining maximum fitness. The lessons draw upon the most effective elements of many different disciplines, including Hatha Yoga, ballet, modern dance and isometrics. The Body Express is expanding soon to include another entire floor with a complete dance supply shop, saunas, an espresso bar and restaurant with a calorie-counted menu.

For Children

Photo: Historical Society of Seattle & King County

I hear you made your goal. Can I have my pledge back?

Seattle listener during KRAB radio marathon

Christopher House

7010 - 35TH AVENUE N.E.
523-9600
HOURS: MONDAY-
SATURDAY 10:15-6:00

If you're the parent of a toddler or two, or a grandma with a long list of underage birthdays . . . and don't know about Christopher House, you haven't done your homework. This is the best source in Seattle for durable, fun and beautiful play equipment and toys. Every item here has to pass the Christopher House test before it goes on the shelf, a standard that assures you each toy is kid-proof and kid-conscious. "Christopher" seems to have a life of its own, nurtured by owner Judy Beuché since its beginnings as a supplier of sturdy, creative play equipment to the nursery school next door. When it comes to describing the selection it's hard to begin. The gallery of teddy bears is a good start. Christopher House has every size and shape of bear from the 1 inch wooden models by Sturges of England to the glorious Riding Bear by Steiff. The bears keep good company with a large irresistable zoo of stuffed animals. European imports include fascinating Brio trains and accessories from Sweden, highly glossed enameled pull toys by Kouvalis, Ambi plastic toys from Holland, Castillos castle building sets from Spain, children's furniture and design toys from Italy, and brightly colored modeling clay from Germany. That list doesn't begin to cover the array of playthings, games, music boxes, doll furniture, and holiday toys and a marvelous collection of handcrafted rocking horses from $65 to $2000. The collection of children's books is in a room of its own and ranges from cloth books for toddler's to complete sets of "The Chronicles of Narnia" by C.S. Lewis. The personal service at this store never stops. They also offer gift wrapping and daily UPS delivery service.

The Linen Orchard

**1134 - 20TH AVENUE E.
SEATTLE, WASHINGTON 98112
(206) 329-8029
PLEASE CALL FOR AN APPOINTMENT.**

The Linen Orchard is the best thing to come along since the bedtime story. This Seattle-based company imports English hand-printed personalized pillowcases for children. Decorated with enchanting animal motifs in the style of old children's book illustrations, they are wonderful gifts for birthdays, Christmas, Easter, or anytime. The pillowcases have been so popular that the designs are now available on hot water bottle covers, toy bags and other accessories. They are meticulously printed in full color on no-iron cotton/polyester blend. The Linen Orchard started out as the idea of Seattleite Kathryn Buchanan and her partner who lives in an orchard in England. It has since grown into a national mail-order business. The designs are all Linen Orchard originals, depicting horses, night owls, sleepy rabbits, honey-thieving bears . . . even parachuting baby chicks, and include a space where the Linen Orchard prints a child's name or a special date. For a catalogue of the complete line, send a stamped, self-addressed envelope. Everything they make comes with a generous supply of sweet dreams.

Magic Mouse Toys

217 FIRST AVE. S.
682-8097
HOURS: MONDAY-THURSDAY
10:00 A.M.-5:30 P.M.
FRIDAY 10:00 A.M.-9:00 P.M.
SUNDAY 12 NOON-5:00 P.M.

The Magic Mouse is the Mercedes of toy stores. In fact, one Seattle group calls it the store for gifted children. It's the only toy store we know of that's run by a professional child. The Child and her fantasy advisor, Gilbert H. Gorilla, Ph.D., are quick to point out that running the store isn't all child's play — it takes a little magic, too. And that's just what you find at the Magic Mouse. Every nook and cranny of this children's fantasy is filled with whimsical toys from around the world and famous brands that have been collectors' items for years. The store is home to every critter from moose to mice, including Steiff bears (the original teddys), purring panthers, unicorns, a bear who sings in High German, and Coco Lapin, the notorious hand-kissing rabbit puppet. You'll also find Coron d'Ache colored pencils, Brio wooden trains and educational toys that make learning fun. The store is easy to find, right across the street from the Grand Central Arcade in Pioneer Square. So satisfy your childish desires. Visit the Magic Mouse.
Visa. Master Charge. American Express.

Alligator Tooth Popsicles
A Children's Bookstore

901 - 19TH AVENUE E.
325-0704
HOURS: TUESDAY-SATURDAY 10:00-6:00

Alligator Tooth Popsicles, believe it or not, is a Capitol Hill bookstore. The name comes from a recipe for Alligator Tooth Popsicles, created by owner Ruth Quinet's son Derrick and it perfectly conveys the flavor of this place. The selection spans the age and interest range from pre-school toddlers to high school age. It's an ambitious scope requiring shrewd understanding of children's needs and tastes, but this delightful store pulls it off very competently. The space is limited, so the emphasis is on fiction, but science, poetry, music, and reference materials are well represented too. Records, tapes, activity and specialty books are also available. Alligator Tooth Popsicles has a funny name, but a serious purpose . . . to provide children with the best available literature, from classic fairy tales to the best in modern fiction. Prices start at 59 cents, not much for investing in a child's reading experience. Extra services include children's accounts, gift certificates, special ordering, a newsletter, and even an occasional storytime on Saturday.

Seattle's Child

P.O. BOX 15107
523-4619
SUBSCRIPTIONS: $9 PER YEAR
$16 FOR 2 YEARS

This is the age of the specialty magazine. Every coffee table in town has some focus, be it sailing, fashion, running, architecture, or people. What about kids, our own children? *Seattle's Child* is an attractive monthly publication, a specialty magazine, but not designed for a stint on the coffee table; rather, to be read and used. The pioneers, Ann Bergman and Sonia Cole created this magazine to meet the need for information on things to do with kids. From circus parades and puppet shows to the best pumpkin picking, their pull-out centerfold calendar opens up a whole new city for parents and children. There are art projects by Diane Katsiaficas, with easy step-by-step directions that encourage parent and child to work together. There's a section reviewing children's and parent's books, another suggesting places to go, like bike rides, discovery trips, and restaurants that welcome families. The consumer column focuses on inexpensive items for children, and the classified section is extremely helpful. Contributing authors include childcare professionals, pediatricians and educators as well as parents, and their articles provide stimulating perspectives on parenting. *Seattle's Child* is a useful and sincere publication that will make you question the value of some of your other subscriptions.

Dan Lambirth Cartoons

317 - 1ST AVENUE S.
PIONEER SQUARE
622-4589
HOURS: 10:00 AM-8:00 PM

Dan Lambirth understands what kids want: they like furniture scaled down to their size, with their name on it so the world has no doubt who owns it, and it's even better if it's decorated with a lot of great colors and maybe made into the shape of their favorite cartoon character or fantasy hero. Dan makes stuff just like that at his Pioneer Square workshop and kids are crazy about it. So are adults as a matter of fact, and the grown-up orders Dan gets would seem to indicate that they're not in the least ashamed to own Raggedy Ann & Andy book ends. The available items include chairs, tables, bookshelves, stepstools, clothes trees, wall coatracks, headboards and toyboxes. A former graphic designer, Dan Lambirth gives each piece a life of its own, embellishing it with a form or face of almost every childhood character there ever was. He's even created some of his own characters and is also able to decorate pieces to match the wallpaper or curtains you already have. He's done special orders for all kinds of people and places, like the toybox he made as a replica of the Medic One van for a doctor's office. Each piece is personalized for its lucky recipient, and best of all, it's very reasonably priced. Constructed of sturdy three-quarter inch plywood, Don Lambirth's Cartoon furniture is made with care and built to last. Please allow 45 days for completion of special orders.

Antiques

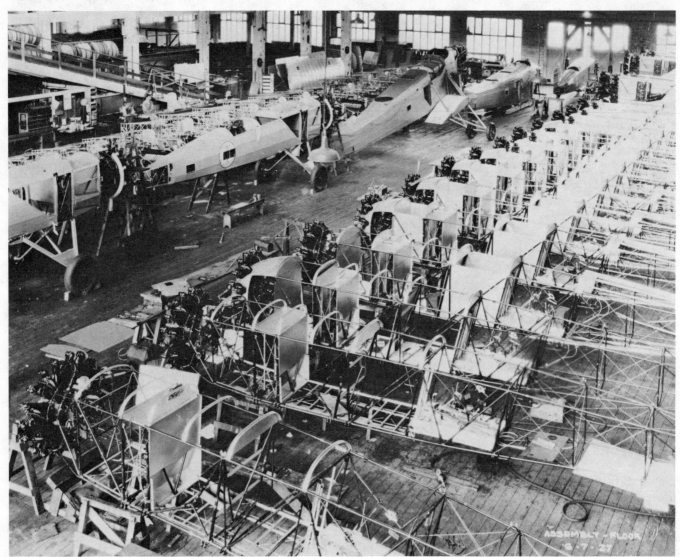

Photo: Historical Society of Seattle & King County

I felt good about the city of Seattle from the day I moved there. It's the only place I know where rich old Republicans aren't always making speeches about how hard-pressed they are.

Bill Russel

The Globe
Antique Shops

529 PINE ST. AT SIXTH AVENUE
682-1420
HOURS: MONDAY-SATURDAY 10:00-5:30

1524 EAST OLIVE WAY
AT EAST DENNY WAY
329-5666
HOURS: TUESDAY-SATURDAY 10:00-5:30

Globe Antiques is considered the best all-around antique dealer in Seattle. It is a shop filled with once-in-a-lifetime finds: an English Harlequin desk, an old American tavern table, rare and unusual chandeliers. Proprietor Betty Balcom has spent years studying her business and developing the international contacts needed to acquire pieces of rare and exceptional value. Her stock includes furniture, accessories, art, and decorative items from the 17th, 18th and early 19th Centuries. The furniture here glows in mahogany, walnut, and cherry woods from America and Europe . . . armoires, tables, chairs and desks, pieces for every room in the house. Investment-oriented collectors will be interested in the Globe's fine collection of Georgian silver and the impressive inventory of original paintings and antique prints. Porcelain purists will delight in pieces representing the finest craftsmen in the world: Sevres from France, Meissen ware from Germany, and England's Worcester and Chelsea. Globe also features an impressive array of beautiful Chinese export porcelain, as well as snuff boxes, coin purses, small boxes and other smaller select items from the world over. Be sure to ask about particular pieces and periods that interest you. The staff at Globe Antiques are a wealth of information.

Wm. L. Davis

1300 5TH AVENUE
622-0518   622-0519
HOURS: MONDAY-FRIDAY
9:00 A.M.-5:00 P.M.
SATURDAY 9:00 A.M.-12:00 NOON

Wm. L. Davis is a respected Seattle establishment, best known for its fine antique collection. There are, however, many other facets to the company. In fact, Wm. L. Davis is both a complete source of fine furniture and an interior design service. The staff is made up entirely of qualified, experienced designers who bring far more than sales knowledge to serving their clients. They are as thoroughly informed about contemporary furniture as they are experts on antiques. These designers may be consulted about any decorating project, be it one room, the restoration of an entire house, or the complete refurbishment of a suite of offices. Wm. L. Davis represents a number of contemporary furniture lines along with its admirable array of antiques, but alternatives include special orders for specific pieces to fulfill the decorating scheme under consideration. The store on Fifth Avenue is world unto itself . . . three floors of harmoniously grouped vignettes, encompassing the finest new and antique pieces for living rooms, dining rooms, bedrooms and pantries. Other accessories on display are hand-selected from Europe and the Orient . . . clocks, lamps, Oriental porcelain, antique silver and brass that suggest exquisite gifts and finishing touches. To many, this is a place synonymous with elegance and prestige, but those who have visited know that this stature has everything to do with the friendly and gracious personal attention they encountered at Wm. L. Davis.

David Reed Weatherford

Antiques and Interiors

133 - 14TH AVENUE E.
329-6533
HOURS: MONDAY-SATURDAY 9:00-5:00
DOWNTOWN WAREHOUSE:
BY APPOINTMENT ONLY.

David Reed Weatherford is one of the city's leading antique dealers and interior designers. He has been working in the antiques field for over twenty years, and in 1971 purchased a beautiful old Capitol Hill mansion built in 1895. This landmark was extensively remodeled and restored under Mr. Weatherford's supervision, and now houses his fine antique shop and interior design service. Specializing in residential design, Mr. Weatherford also accepts commercial design projects from his varied clientele. These projects have included offices, retirement homes and retail shops such as the recently completed Fox's Gem Shop. In addition to his many Washington clients, Mr. Weatherford has also undertaken design and decorating projects for people in California and Europe. The shop itself is a marvel. It houses the collection of 17th, 18th, and 19th Century Georgian, French and Italian furniture, a good selection of small antique objects and accessories, many Oriental art and porcelain pieces, as well as Oriental screens from the 17th and 18th Centuries. Smaller items include beautiful primitive African art, Northwest Indian baskets, and Egyptian and Etruscan artifacts. The owner's experience and knowledge is varied; he is well known for his talents in combining different styles and periods to achieve distinctive interiors of enduring elegance.

Master Charge. BankAmericard.

Sixth Avenue Antiques

1330 SIXTH AVENUE
622-1110
HOURS: MONDAY-SATURDAY 10:00-5:30

Provincial and useful seems to be the theme at Sixth Avenue Antiques where they feature country antiques from the manor homes, farm houses, and estates of 18th and 19th Century France and England. The owners, Bob Alsin and Jean Williams, make several buying trips a year to Europe. What they have learned in 30 years of buying, selling, and interior design makes this shop one that gives the customer a particular sense of confidence and trust. They're specialists in room arrangements and the art of combining antiques with your present decor or lifestyle, whether you live in a manor home or condominium. At Sixth Avenue Antiques there is a large selection of French armoires, tables, and sets of chairs. From the British Isles, chests of drawers, Welsh dressers, drop leaf tables, Windsor chairs, and a variety of desks are in stock. There's something romantic about the life that used to center around the fireplace, an area that gets ample attention here. You'll find Seattle's largest collection of antique and handcarved fire mantles, fire fenders, andirons, sets of tools, and coal boxes. Sixth Avenue Antiques has a special preview party for customers when each new shipment arrives from Europe. So, much like the British used to celebrate when tea and spices arrived from the Far East, there's an opportunity here to marvel at the latest tea chests in town. It's a wonderful way to stay informed on the antique market in the city.
Visa. Master Charge.

Honeychurch Antiques

2604 - 3RD AVENUE
OLD VINE COURT
SEATTLE
622-1225
HOURS: MONDAY-SATURDAY 10:00-6:00

29 HOLLYWOOD ROAD
HONG KONG
(5) 432-433
HOURS: EVERYDAY 10:00-6:00

John and Laurie Fairman are the proprietors of Honeychurch Antiques, Seattle. Anyone who has ever visited the shop comes away full of praise for these two charming people. It's hard to imagine more congenial attention than you will receive at their shop. Specializing in fine antiques and folk crafts from Asian countries, the Seattle shop is in fact a branch of Honeychurch Hong Kong, begun by Mr. and Mrs. Glenn Vessa in 1963. Honeychurch Seattle is located in the lovely Old Vine Court, a two-storey brick building on Third Avenue. They have a representative selection of 18th and 19th Century furniture, ceramics, fabrics, prints, paintings and jewelry from all over the Orient. After a few minutes in the shop, it is obvious that the Vessas have done their collecting well. Discriminating collectors and browsers are always welcome . . . all are treated graciously. The Fairmans enjoy telling the fascinating stories about the objects that have come through history to Honeychurch Antiques. Visa. Master Charge.

Porter Davis

**607 UNION STREET
622-5310
HOURS: MONDAY-SATURDAY 10:30-5:30
11138 GRAVELLY LAKE DRIVE S.W.
TACOMA
588-8085
HOURS: MONDAY-SATURDAY 10:30-5:30**

If you can't find a certain antique, chances are Porter Davis can find it for you. Porter Davis is one of Seattle's outstanding antique galleries. They specialize in fine quality 18th and early 19th Century English, French and American furniture, silver, porcelain, decorative accessories, paintings and Oriental rugs. Owner Jenkins Henslee is well-versed in his field, and is a veritable Sherlock Holmes when it comes to tracking down particular pieces for his clients. Searches are thorough and professional, using all the resources available to locate fine examples of a particular period or style. Porter Davis has an impressive collection of stock on hand. The gallery also offers professional appraisal service. Porter Davis's original store is in Lakewood, and is known for its relaxed, rural atmosphere.
Visa. Master Charge.

Barker's Antiques

**22456 PACIFIC HIGHWAY S.
878-4161
PLEASE TELEPHONE FOR AN
APPOINTMENT.**

Barker's Antiques specializes in only the finest European and American antiques. Established in 1938, the shop enjoys a solid reputation for quality in Seattle. Owner Vianna Barker Kelly is a certified member of Appraiser's Association of America and does appraisals of fine art, antiques and jewelry. Nationally respected in her field, she is often called on to appraise entire estates. With such expertise and knowledge at her disposal, it stands to reason that she would only carry the best, and so she does. You'll find a wide range of art glass like Tiffany, Steuben, Bohemian glass, Burmese glass and Cameo glass; Tiffany lamps, silver, European and American bowls and tableware, and furniture as well. Her antique jewelry is especially fine . . . rarities from antique coral and Victorian jewelry to rose diamonds and antique watches. An added attraction is her selection of reference books on antiques — many of them are hard-to-find publications, which any lover of antiques will cherish.

Vanishing Art et Cie.

1927-1929 - 1ST AVENUE
624-2252
HOURS: TUESDAY-SATURDAY 10:00-5:00
OR BY APPOINTMENT.

Jiri Osers and Isobel Carr-Johnson have been acquiring fine Asian art and antiques for 15 years, and the pieces from their collection available for sale at Vanishing Art et Cie. are a superb reflection of their knowledge of the field. This is the kind of specialty enterprise that until recently could only be found in New York or London. Housed in an attractive space on First Avenue near Pike Place Market, these pieces represent the best of Chinese, Japanese and Southeast Asian art; many dating as far back as the 8th Century. Vanishing Art et Cie. sells to clients all over the world, including many museums. They conduct world-wide searches as well, to locate particular pieces their clients have requested. The owners may be consulted about collecting for investment, and appraisals are available for major pieces.

Michael Andersen Antiques/ Interiors

**208 S. MAIN STREET AT SECOND AVE.
PIONEER SQUARE
623-9231
HOURS: TUESDAY-SATURDAY 12:00-5:00
MORNINGS BY APPOINTMENT**

This is one of Seattle's newest sources for fine antiques. Michael Andersen sells quality period furniture from a beautiful restored space in the Pioneer Square area. The shop specializes in fine 18th and 19th Century French and Italian furniture and accessories, and indeed this is the first shop to focus almost exclusively on this branch of the antique field. Michael comes to antique dealing from a background in Interior Design, and offers complete design services to clients who feel that investment in furniture of this calibre deserves attention to placement in the home and harmonious coordination with other facets of design. Michael has accordingly included antique pieces from other cultures and periods in this collection, such as Oriental porcelain and screens. There is a restoration service for period pieces which naturally specializes in the antiques most familiar to the business. The collection here is constantly changing but always impressive. Some discoveries might include a Louis XV bench, an Empire chaise lounge, a Louis XVI trumeau mirror with original oil painting, a magnificent Régence caned arm chair, a Provincial buffet à deux corps, a Louis XVI fall front desk, elegant little Venetian foot stools and much more. Michael Andersen is also proud to represent the contemporary wood sculpture of Roberto Tacchi.

Mariko Tada

6TH AND OLIVE
624-7667
HOURS: MONDAY-SATURDAY 9:30-5:30

Mariko Tada is a place of real discovery. This fine art gallery, established in Seattle in 1968, deals exclusively and expertly in Asian art — primarily Japanese, Chinese and Korean ceramics. The collection also includes choice examples of netsuke, snuff bottles, jade and other small art objects, ranging in age from archaic to 19th Century. Drawing on an extensive and carefully developed contacts in London, New York and Tokyo-Kyoto, the dealers at Mariko Tada are able to acquire some of the finest existing examples of Asian art for their clients. Indeed, special searches for particular objects are an invited challenge. Private collectors and many American museums have located major acquisitions with Mariko Tada's help. The gallery offers ceramic restorations to both regular clients and public institutions; one of the few sources here for such work. Due to the exacting nature of this skill and great demand for it, jobs often require three to six months to complete. Written Appraisals and documentation of Asian art is another service and a complete rate schedule is available at Mariko Tada.

Dale Rutherford's
Third Hand Shop

11 W. McGRAW
284-3011
HOURS: 12:00-6:00 SEVEN DAYS A WEEK

If you'd like a friend in the antique business, meet Dale Rutherford, owner of the Third Hand Shop. His large blue French house on top of Queen Anne has become a landmark for antique hunters and the door is open seven days a week. Inside, you'll find three floors crammed with Dale's finds from trips throughout the United States and Europe. There are wooden file cabinets, rolltop desks, armoires, wicker chairs, wood chairs, round oak tables and fine furniture from Europe. Lanterns, baskets and antique bird cages hang from the ceiling . . . the walls are a wealth of old pictures, mirrors, clocks and plates. One room in the Third Hand Shop features things for the kitchen: pastry tables, crocks, copper boilers and kitchen queens. Other rooms overflow with brass and copper items, old baskets and lamps. The shop also reflects Dale's interest in refurbishing old homes, with a wide selection of stained and beveled glass windows, oak toilet seats and tanks, light fixtures and fireplace mantles. So when all the dust settles and you're still searching for just the right antique, take heart. The Third Hand Shop on Queen Anne Hill is waiting to give you a hand.

 # Oasis

Antique Oriental Rugs

5655 UNIVERSITY WAY N.E.
525-2060
HOURS: MONDAY-SATURDAY 11:00-6:00

Nothing can give a room quite the same presence and elegance as an antique Oriental rug. It is at once the most basic and yet opulent furnishing of all. Oasis Antique Oriental Rugs has a selection that can impart the flavor of just about every exotic culture in the Orient. Douglas Barnhart houses his collection in a lovely space in the University District that feels more like a gallery than a shop. Here you will find one of the Northwest's leading array of rugs from ancient Persia, China, Turkey and Central Asia, beautifully displayed for your perusal. Made by village and nomadic weavers, from 50 to 150 years ago, these rich and vibrant creations are lifelong investments. Mr. Barnhart has spent 10 years amassing this collection and also offers his skills in appraising, buying and brokering antique Persian and Oriental rugs. Aptly named, this establishment *is* a charming oasis, and a doorway into another world.

Wicker Design

515 - 15TH AVE. E., CAPITOL HILL
322-2552
HOURS: WEDNESDAY-SATURDAY
12:00-5:00
OR BY APPOINTMENT

They don't serve mint juleps at Wicker Design, but the feeling of southern aristocratic leisure fans its way throughout this very specialized antique store. Original and restored wicker furniture is the trade here. One important source is the deep south. Owner Alan Serebrin buys American pieces and one-of-a-kind collectors items in Louisville, Nashville, and makes other stops on the southern auction route. He also finds a rich offering locally of wicker furniture from individuals and antique dealers. Couches, chairs, love seats, desks, day beds . . . they're all original; no reproductions. Exotic platform rockers, fringe lamps, rolled wicker, intricate tables are just part of the inventory. Pieces dating from pre-civil war days up to the 1920's are all in peach condition because of the expert restoration service. If your old wicker rocker has a hole in it and a complex from being turned down by every repair shop in town, bring it here. It will be rehabilitated. Because Alan is such an active wicker hunter with an extensive network of sources he encourages special requests. He'll do his best to find that one piece needed for the garden room, solarium or budding collection.

The Oak Emporium

8005 GREENWOOD AVENUE N.
783-5040
HOURS: TUESDAY-SATURDAY 11:00-6:00
SUNDAY 11:00-5:00
CLOSED MONDAY

When you know what you want, and you want oak
. . . here it is. The Oak Emporium has one of
Seattle's largest selections of old furniture in
beautiful condition. Collectors of oak come here for
the extensive array of tables, chairs, desks, beds,
plant stands, armoires and wardrobes. Many
pieces have been professionally restored by experts
at the Oak Emporium, taking pains to maintain the
original beauty of the wood. The Oak Emporium
also has antique pieces in a variety of other fine

woods . . . mahogany, walnut, and cherry. Most of
the stock comes from England or America, and there
are unusual finds in every corner. The stock here is
constantly changing, so it's a wonderful place for
treasure hunting. If you have oak furniture that
needs restoration the staff at the Oak Emporium can
have been doing it for years and can tell you
precisely how to go about it.
Visa. Master Charge.

B. Gorlick & Son Antiques

1914 3RD AVENUE
622-4090
HOURS: MONDAY- SATURDAY 9:30-5:30

B. Gorlick and Son Antiques is one of those places where you will find exactly what you've been searching for and much more. It's a treasure-hunter's delight. Some of the most predictable finds are porcelain, ivory and stone carvings, and lacquer from the Orient; military collectibles like old guns, swords, uniforms and medals; nautical curios, clocks and telescopes; Indian and Eskimo carvings, rugs, baskets and ivory. There are collectors' items for virtually every kind of collection, be it butterflies, shells, minerals, stamps or coins, old prints, manuscripts, ancient artifacts, engravings and paintings . . . plus that unexpected, serendipitous find sure to be tucked around the corner somewhere at B. Gorlick and Son Antiques.

Broadway Clock Shop

618 BROADWAY E.
(CAPITOL HILL)
322-3022
HOURS: MONDAY-
SATURDAY 9:30-6:30

If you prefer clocks that tick and chime to those that hum and buzz, visit the Broadway Clock Shop. Located in the Capitol Hill shopping district, the Broadway Clock Shop is a refuge for anyone who admires quality craftsmanship. The store features an international selection of mantle, wall and tallcase clocks as well as a sampling of fine pocket watches. Owners Michael Larson and Roger Hewat are eager to share their knowledge with collectors and browsers alike, so don't hesitate to ask questions. The shop offers a complete repair service with all work fully guaranteed. Delivery and installation is free with every sale. In addition, they welcome the opportunity to buy and trade mechanical clocks of all kinds.
Visa. Master Charge. BankAmericard

Lambda Shop Antiques

at Wick's

**1658 E. OLIVE WAY
HOURS: TUESDAY-
SATURDAY 9:00-5:00
324-7676**

**600 E. PINE STREET
HOURS: MONDAY-
SATURDAY 12:00-6:00
323-5120**

As you enter Lambda Shop Antiques your ears immediately tune to the gentle ticking of dozens of old wall clocks, your feet move quietly over handmade carpets and your eyes glide from brass beds to oak tables to marbletop washstands. Whether buying or just browsing, this place is a pleasure . . . Lambda has a diversity and price range that's hard to beat. The shop was started by manager David Neth with two thoughts foremost, that the shop be owned and operated as a fund-raiser for the 6-year-old Gay Community Center and that it should not be necessary to make a week's profit on the sale of one item. In December of 1978 a second location was opened at Wick's Hair Art across from the Henry's Off Broadway. Its high ceiling accommodates a number of larger pieces, as well as other items similar to the selection at the main shop. A second-generation clock repair person works out of the main shop.
Visa. Master Charge.

For the Home

Photo: Historical Society of Seattle & King County

I often think of you there in Seattle: clouds gathered over head, skins pasty and mole-like, the grey winds of the north leaning down to chill the bone and darken the soul. I think of that, and my soft political heart goes out to you.

Richard A.C. Green, who ran for Washington State Land Commissioner while lounging around on the beach in Hawaii.

Cap'n Sam's Loft

2702 - 1ST AVENUE S.
624-1478
HOURS: MONDAY-
SATURDAY 11:00-6:00

Cap'n Sam's Loft has the largest supply of antique and used building materials in the city. This huge facility houses 4 floors full of furniture and covers 90,000 square feet. Most of the stock comes from somewhere in the Seattle area and includes every kind of furniture and fixture item anyone would ever need. In vintage light fixtures alone, the inventory exceeds 5,000 pieces. What makes this place so special is that Cap'n Sam's does all their own salvaging to ensure that everything is in the best possible condition for re-use. You can call to see what they've got if you're after something in particular, or make a visit to hunt for doors and windows; old cornices, archways, banisters and columns; bathroom fixtures, furniture, a myriad of smaller items . . . and antique clocks in every size from mantle-piece models to stately grandfathers. These days, the collection includes the Pierce County Courthouse doors, and even an entire Victorian elevator salvaged from the State Capitol Building in Helena, Montana, in case that's just the thing you've been searching for.
Visa. Master Charge.

 # Bushell's Auction

2006 - 2ND AVENUE
622-5833
HOURS: MONDAY-FRIDAY
8:00 A.M.-5:00 P.M.
MONDAY 8:00 A.M.-7:00 P.M.
FOR PREVIEWING
TUESDAY — AUCTION DAY

Bushell's Auction House is a living chapter of Seattle history that is still going strong. It was established in 1908 by John Bushell, who arrived in Seattle in 1889 with 35¢ in his pocket. The business is still carried on, four generations later, by the Bushell family. It is still the leading auction house in Seattle. Auctions are held just about every Tuesday, starting at 9 a.m. and last as long as the merchandise does. You'll find almost anything imaginable on the block at any given time . . . funky junk to treasured antiques. Bushell's frequently handles estate auctions, selling entire housefuls of old and new objects. The commission is 40% on items sold for less than $50 and 20% on anything bringing more. Unlike other auction houses, Bushell's has no "reserve pricing", which means that no item has a minimum affixed price before it goes up for bid. Whatever price an object fetches from the assembled bidders is what it goes for. John Bushell put it succinctly years ago: "You either run an auction house or a retail store." Bushell's definitely runs an auction house.

Pande Cameron & Company of Seattle

815 PINE STREET
624-6263
HOURS: MONDAY-
FRIDAY 9:00-5:30
SATURDAY 10:00-4:00

When you have decided to invest in a fine Oriental carpet, you want only the best. Pande Cameron is where you'll find it. And when you are looking for quality, but don't necessarily want to break the bank to get it, Pande Cameron is still the place to go. The Andonian family has been importing exquisite hand-made rugs from all over the world since 1924, and they have one of the foremost collections on the West Coast . . . everything from collector's items that rival museum-quality art to durable, practical and beautiful rugs that represent the best value for your money. Pande Cameron carries only natural fibre carpets, both wool and silk, which they personally select from the Middle East, China, India and even Eastern Europe. Deservedly proud of their knowledge and experience, the Andonians are always willing to spend time with first-time buyers as well as seasoned collectors, helping to make the right choice. As any good collector can tell you, Pande Cameron is also the place to entrust your Oriental rugs for cleaning and repair. The service and care is unmatched.

Swanson's

9701 15TH AVE. N.W.
782-2543
HOURS: MONDAY-SUNDAY 9:30-6:00

Swanson's is a greenthumber's paradise. It is Seattle's premiere plant, gift and garden center, with four acres of grounds and nursery stock and 17 greenhouses. The thousands of plants and flowers here are personally grown or handpicked by Swanson's, the quality would make any gardener green with envy. Each plant has everything an expert looks for: vivid color, lush growth and the potential of becoming a garden showpiece. Swanson's staggering variety includes every plant you've ever heard of, and a good many you haven't. But it's the way the plants are displayed that really makes Swanson's special. The nursery is overflowing with beautiful ideas for gardens, patios, pot arrangements and hanging baskets. Swanson's features handmade surprises for every holiday season, and the annual Christmas open house is something you won't want to miss. It starts early in November and attracts thousands of people from all over the Northwest. Of course, Swanson's is at its blooming best in the spring, a botanical wonderland of greenery, bedding plants and blossoms. If you have a question or need help planning a garden, just ask. Swanson's friendly and knowledgeable staff is just one more reason why this nursery has been a perennial favorite of Seattle's gardeners for 91 years.
Visa. Master Charge.

Draheim & Partners

305 6TH & PINE BLDG.
623-4888
HOURS: MONDAY-FRIDAY 9:00-5:00

Interior design and space planning . . . one service doesn't come without the other from Draheim & Partners, a name that has become closely associated with an intelligent, contemporary approach to the design profession. This firm's attitude dispels any notion that the only thing interior designers do is tell you which sofa to choose. Partners Terris Draheim, Susan Okamoto and Linda Popp attach the same importance to spatial planning as they do to design. Their considerations focus on the parameters, possibilities and limitations of a space. Choices in lighting, furnishings, fabrics and finishing touches should all enhance the inherent qualities of the space. Their success has much to do with their team approach. They work to combine their different areas of expertise, resources and outlooks, because they have found this to be the best way of arriving at a final look and life of a space that truly accommodates their clients' needs. It is a sensible system where attention to the circumstances of each project plays a decisive role in finding the appropriate response. Draheim & Partners undertakes both residential and commercial projects, and excell at devising solutions to situations where budget limitations have created a problem. As they put it, "Good design doesn't just happen . . . you have to *make* it happen." They do.

Jean Jongeward

**119 TOWER PLACE
SEATTLE
284-1999
HOURS: MONDAY-FRIDAY 9:00-5:00**

Experience is only one of the reasons why Jean Jongeward is respected and admired in the community of Northwest designers. She has consistently displayed her gift for innovation and her dedication to the concept of total design. It is because of this integration of design (color, materials, and space) that Jean frequently works with architects during the initial phase of designing residential or commercial space, her work reflecting the image of the entire structure. She is distinctly sensitive to the wants and needs of her clients, and carefully co-ordinates the lifestyle or business pattern of each. Custom-design furnishings are created with a preference for natural fabrics, often complemented by modern metal or plastic pieces with a classic look that is timeless. Jean Jongeward's flair for contemporary ideas is equalled by her extensive knowledge of antiques: she selected all the antique furnishings for the Governor's mansion in Olympia. Her work is known nationally through features in such respected publications as House and Garden, Architectural Digest, and Interior Designs.

©Dick Busher 1979

William Overholt,
A.S.I.D.

1902 - 10TH EAST
323-7223
HOURS: MONDAY-FRIDAY 9:00-5:00

The most beautiful homes in Seattle are extensions of the natural Northwest environment. In that sense, interior designer William Overholt is one of Seattle's leading environmentalists. Mr. Overholt works out of a studio in his Capitol Hill home. The home itself is a confident expression of the owner's philosophy, and has been featured in both local and international publications. Mr. Overholt's interiors exude an ambiance of understated elegance, comfort and natural beauty. Each setting is a carefully balanced ecosystem of contemporary and antique furniture, complemented with natural fibers such as wools, cottons and linens. Custom design furniture also plays an important part in the total interior design effect that Mr. Overholt creates. His concepts are enthusiastically embraced by homeowners both locally and nationally. For many, he has made the country's most livable homes even more livable.

Keeg's

310 BROADWAY AVENUE E.
325-1771
HOURS: MONDAY 9:00 A.M.-9:00 P.M.
TUESDAY-SATURDAY 9:00 A.M.-5:30 P.M.

Keeg's is that big blue store on Broadway that's always filled with wonderful things. Furniture, area rugs, dinnerware, toys, jewelry, leather goods, kitchen items, crystal, cards, fine soaps and bubble bath, mirrors, linens, picture frames, cards and wrapping paper — it's all here, and the one unifying feature in this outstanding array is beautiful design.

If it doesn't function terrifically and look wonderful, you won't find it at Keeg's. Owner Walter Kerr looks to sources all over the world to come up with a combination of functional and fascinating items. The shop itself is large and comfortable, with striking displays and easy access to everything. There's plenty of space to sit down and try out a chair, or test out a handy little Sabina carpet-sweeper ideally designed for entrance hall touch-ups. Downstairs holds lots more furniture, and the ''Discovery Shop'' where Keeg's has placed all the uncategorizable oddments that stimulate the imagination . . . each the perfect choice for one single person in the whole world. Keeg's has a catalog division for mail-order needs and a friendly, knowledgeable sales staff to help you.
Visa. Master Charge. American Express.

Sujo's

1716 EAST OLIVE WAY (across from Henry's)
325-5350
HOURS: MONDAY-SATURDAY 10:00-5:30
10245 MAIN STREET
MAIN PLACE MALL
BELLEVUE
454-3350
HOURS: MONDAY-SATURDAY 10:00-6:00

In a city that is literally crawling with design stores, Susan Johnston runs two shops that easily walk off with the honors. The Capitol Hill Sujo's looks deceptively small, but inside it climbs to three levels and carries a better stock than many larger places. The shop in Bellevue's Main Place is larger and features the same quality lines. The emphasis is on contemporary home and office furnishings and accessories that are well-designed, functional, beautiful and affordable. That sounds like a rare combination, but Susan has gathered an array of products and lines that fill the bill. Look for lighting from Luxo, Keystone and Basic Concept; furniture by Emu, Sherwood and Innovator; and accessories and bath products by Crayonne, Beylerian/Kartell, Wings and IDG. There's always a great selection of the popular Finnish fabric line, Marimekko, as well as lots of other fine products, presented with the kind of flair and panache Sujo's is known for.
Visa. Master Charge.

McBreen

905 E. JOHN STREET
ON CAPITOL HILL JUST OFF BROADWAY
323-2336
HOURS: MONDAY-SATURDAY 9:00-5:30

Sometimes, after an interior designer gets through with your house, it feels like you're living in a department store window. That's a situation that the designers at McBreen scrupulously avoid. They're concerned with creating spaces especially for you . . . spaces you can be proud of yet still feel comfortable living in. The staff at McBreen is composed of professional qualified interior designers who work closely with each client,

combining existing furnishings and accessories with new pieces to achieve a tasteful, natural, "non-decorated" look. They'll find imaginative ways to combine antiques with contemporary pieces. McBreen has been a leading interior design outlet for nearly 30 years, and has access to all major manufacturers of furniture and accessories from all over the United States and the world. The latest in European designer lines are available, of course, but their buyer travels constantly in search of the extraordinary, which "en masse" in the shop look like something akin to a Turkish bazaar. McBreen is known to have one of the city's finer collections of lamps, beautiful imported and domestic handcrafted baskets, and other items for the home . . . from mirrors and wall hangings to fine Oriental porcelain, as well as a limited collection of select antiques.
Visa. Master Charge.

Egbert's

2231 1ST AVENUE
624-3377
HOURS: MONDAY-SATURDAY 9:30-6:00

Egbert's is named for owner Jim Egbert, a co-founder of Keeg's on Broadway, one of Seattle's first design-oriented stores. Jim's experience and knowledge find full expression in his latest successful project, a new store in Belltown. Egbert's pays no attention to trendy brands or prices, so you'll find everything from $1 wine glasses to $2,500 rugs . . . and things you can't find anywhere else at that. The criteria for choosing stock are simply good design and quality. Everything in the store is personally selected by Jim Egbert, during two annual trips to Europe, New York and Los Angeles. While you'll certainly find many popular quality lines, it's the limited-quantity treasures that make the store exciting. The space is large enough to comfortably accommodate a selection of furniture, lamps and lighting, rugs, tableware, kitchenware, toys, natural fibre textiles for every room, paper products, candles and more. The displays are always entertaining . . . a pleasingly clever touch that tells you a lot about Egbert's sense of design.
Visa. Master Charge.

Feathered Friends

2130 - 1ST AVENUE
622-0974
HOURS: MONDAY-FRIDAY 10:30-5:30
SATURDAY 11:00-5:00
OR BY APPOINTMENT

1314 N.E. 43RD STREET
632-4402
HOURS: MONDAY-FRIDAY 9:00-4:30

Feathered Friends is a shop dedicated to keeping people warm. To that end, this friendly place not only sells but actually manufactures, beautiful down comforters and pillows, because they want to make sure that it's done right. Owners Carol Yeatts and Peter Hickner began by making sleeping bags, and they did that so well that three of their sleeping bags have been rated "best in the country" by *Backpacker* magazine. That same workmanship goes into their delightfully pretty and warm comforters. Available in a wide range of sizes and prices, the comforters come in two basic models: the traditional Channeled Style and the cosier, more expensive European. In either case, only the finest quality mature, cold-climate goose down goes into them, and they're sewn so that there are never any thinly-filled cold spots . . . just nice, fluffy warmth all over. They are truly deluxe. Feathered Friends makes sheet case covers too, and everything's available through mail-order, and fully guaranteed. Visa. Master Charge.

Aria Carpets

**409 MAIN STREET
EDMONDS, WASHINGTON 98020
(206)776-2454
HOURS: TUESDAY-SATURDAY 10:00-5:00**

Carolynne Harris' interest in Persian carpets began during the time her family spent living in Tehran, Iran. While there, she made an extensive study of the art and travelled to Shiraza and Isfahan, two important rugmaking centers, to observe craftsmen at work. That rich experience has resulted in her lovely Edmonds shop where she sells new Persian rugs of the finest quality. Named for the ancient word for Persia, Aria Carpets carries a stock of several hundred investment-quality carpets that increase in value tremendously every year you own them. In fact, every selection includes Carolynne's guarantee to buy back any carpet at the original purchase price. Carolynne knows her field well; she's familiar with the colors and designs of both city and tribal Persian rugs. These hand-knotted carpets are all made of wool, wool and silk, or pure silk. Carolynne feels that the real secret to getting the best rugs is to identify the leading sources and deal exclusively with them, which is exactly what she does.

Visa. Master Charge.

 # Old & Elegant Distributing

10203 MAIN STREET LANE
BELLEVUE
455-4660
HOURS: MONDAY-SATURDAY 10:00-6:00
THURSDAY UNTIL 9:00

If you're remodeling or building your dream home from the ground up, Old & Elegant Distributing is a place you should know about. This place carries the kind of designer and construction specialty items that you've always thought they didn't make anymore. For starters, they have the Northwest's largest collection of solid brass bath fixtures, with coordinating towel racks and other companion hardware. Some are antique and some feature designs created by owners Dennis and Jean True. Their shop is also the sole source locally for Venetian marble fixtures . . . sunken tubs, lavatory tops, tub and shower wall panels, fireplace facings, hearths and table tops. Before you buy just any old sink, you ought to look into the very special selection at Old & Elegant . . . decorated china, pottery and metal, in over 100 designs. And, for one of our more unusual specialties, are you ready for the Northwest's largest collection of weather vanes? Then there are hand-made tiles, etched glass windows, terracotta wall friezes, carved doors, and lighting fixtures. For the collector, there's even solid gold and platinum antique jewelry and art glass, stowed away in a vault that was at one time the first bank in Bellevue. The Trues encourage their customers to handle and touch the items they are viewing to appreciate the rich textures in this interesting collection.

Capetown Rio

1333 FIFTH AVE., RAINIER SQUARE
622-9373
HOURS: MONDAY-
SATURDAY 9:30-5:30

Capetown Rio's collection of fine linens is a far cry from run-of-the-mill department stores. Embroidered table linen, fashionable sheets from Martex, colorful cotton towels — everything here begs to be touched and treasured. The items includes bath accessories in china, brass, oak and marble, but focuses on home textile products. What unifies the collection is exclusivity: there are custom-designed, hard-to-find imported or handmade items from all over the world . . . including classic collectors' items of investment quality. The fabric items are all natural fiber products of cotton, linen, wool or blends; including bedding, table linen, trousseau items and bath products. You'll find cashmere and wool blankets, dreamy 100% cotton flannel sheets and down bedding to take the chill off Northwest nights. Virtually anything can be special ordered and custom designed — and monogramming is available on most Capetown Rio linens. They even carry a line of natural hand-milled soaps that can be monogrammed to co-ordinate with all your bath accessories. No matter what you buy at Capetown Rio, you can be sure it's quality to the last letter. Visa. Master Charge.

 # International Kitchens

**13500 BEL-RED ROAD
BELLEVUE
641-5363
6501 S.W. 196TH STREET
LYNNWOOD
774-8014
HOURS: MONDAY-FRIDAY 9:00-5:30
SATURDAY 10:00-4:00**

At International Kitchens, the philosophy is that form should follow function beautifully. As professionals in designing, equipping, and installing home kitchens, International's first concern is that a kitchen be convenient and efficient. That is why they offer features such as roll-out shelving, cooking islands, revolving pantries, and concealed fixtures . . . not to mention the most advanced appliances available from Roper, Sub-Zero, Thermador and other fine manufacturers. Efficiency alone, however, is not enough. The kitchen is the heart of the home and it deserves the same attention to decor as any other room. For this reason, International carries only the finest European styles of cabinetry, crafted in Honduras mahogany and oak in five stains, and over one hundred colorful and durable laminates. Whether you are building a new home or remodeling, visit one of International's design centers and discover how beautiful and functional a kitchen can be.

Fabrik

321 BROADWAY AVENUE E.
329-2110
HOURS: MONDAY-FRIDAY 10:00-7:00
SATURDAY 10:00-5:30
SUNDAY 12:00-5:00

You can purchase modern hand-glazed stoneware for 50% less than retail at this wonderful Capitol Hill outlet. The Fabrik seconds store carries slightly irregular pieces of the well-known Fabrik dinnerware that is manufactured right here in Seattle, and sold in fine stores all over the country. If you are curious about their definition of "seconds", take a magnifying glass! The name "fabrik" means a place where objects are made, and it stands for all the hand-processes that go into creating this stoneware. The patterns are inspired by and named for Northwest places, and co-ordinate with each other beautifully. Design purists will appreciate the care that goes into each piece: cups are balanced for easy handling, pieces fit together to expand their uses, and the non-porous, stain-resistant stoneware can be safely used in the oven. Fabrik also carries the best in other Northwest-inspired design products, including Alleniana hand silk-screened fabric from Port Townsend, toys by both the Oregon Wooden Toy Company and Off Center Studio in Seattle, Barry Harems' hand silk-screened Northwest Indian prints, ironworks from Enclume, and handmade Broomtales brooms.
Visa. Master Charge.

Gallery of Kitchens

10129 MAIN STREET
BELLEVUE
453-8903
HOURS: MONDAY-FRIDAY 9:00-5:30
SATURDAY 10:00-4:00

Gallery of Kitchens is a complete kitchen design center featuring the finest in American cabinet makers' art: 42 distinctive cabinetry styles crafted by Medallion and other superior designs. Whether you're involved in new construction or remodeling an old kitchen that never suited you to begin with, you'll be able to choose cabinet designs ranging from traditional to contemporary in oak, cherry, pecan, birch, or pine. The bonus here is that Gallery staff can do the whole job for you . . . from design consultation, right through installation. The total approach is recommended; experience has shown that it usually saves you time, trouble and expense. This outlet carries the best names in kitchen fixtures and appliances, notably Roper, Jenn-Air, Sub-Zero, Thermador, Bendix, Crosley and Waste King. The design professionals at Gallery of Kitchens also help you complete your new kitchen decor with coordinating counter tops, as well as wall and floor finishing with a full range of tile and laminates from Corian and other makers.

Butcherblock Warehouse

320 TERRY AVENUE N.
624-8596
HOURS: MONDAY 10:00-6:00
TUESDAY-FRIDAY 8:00-6:00
SATURDAY 10:00-5:00

Years before high-tech furniture became the rage, there was the butcherblock table, one of the first successes in adapting an industrial design to home decor. It's a trend that has caught on all over the country. The Butcherblock Warehouse in Seattle has taken this good idea one step further and created a whole line of hardwood furniture based on the laminated-wood butcherblock design. This warehouse-sized retail outlet has a strictly no-frills set-up, where all the energy goes into high quality materials, careful workmanship and low cost. There's great variety in size, shape and use, starting with the good old-fashioned meat blocks just like the butchers have; moving on to table tops and pedestals, counter tops, chairs, coffee tables, and some very comfortable sofas with exposed oak-frames in a range of contemporary fabric designs. Only the finest hardwoods are used . . . oak, hardrock maple and European beechwood, giving these pieces durability and a beauty that improves with age. Any purchase may be shipped anywhere. All reflect the Butcherblock Warehouse style — a blend of casual, sophisticated and sturdy good looks.

Visa. Master Charge.

The Woodstove Store and
August West Chimney Sweeps

1316 E. PINE STREET
325-3299
HOURS: WEDNESDAY-SATURDAY
10:00-5:00
THURSDAY UNTIL 8:00

The new Woodstove Store is the logical progression from the August West Chimney Sweeps service, which Carol Anderson and Beliz Brothers started in 1975. A familiar sight on the rooftops of Seattle, Carol and Beliz recently joined with Karen Bosley to open their Capitol Hill outlet for the most energy-efficient, environmentally sound and well-designed wood burning stoves available. They import the original cast-iron Jøtul line from Norway, the wood or coal burning Le Petit Godin from France, the Efel model from Belgium, the Waterford from Ireland, as well as the domestically produced Fisher and Garrison lines. The chimney sweep service is still available and may be arranged through the Woodstove Store. House calls come with important information on fireplace and chimney maintenance. Putting all their experience to work, these three women teach free workshops covering all aspects of woodheating, conducted at community centres and King County libraries. Call the Woodstove Store for schedule information.
Visa. Master Charge.

Al's Easy Livin'

13211 NORTHRUP WAY
BELLEVUE
746-8004, 622-7221
HOURS: MONDAY-FRIDAY 8:00-6:00
SATURDAY 9:00-5:00

We all know that easy livin' can sometimes be downright difficult when the collapsable chairs do nothing but collapse and the swimming pool has turned into a science experiment. That's what Al's Easy Livin' is all about. Everything you need for luxury outdoor living can be found at Al's. First, there's the complete swimming pool and maintenance service, staffed by fully-trained personnel who keep up on the latest developments and techniques for healthy pools. There's a great variety of pool accessories including filters, lighting fixtures, umbrellas, vacuum cleaners, water testing kits, and pool toys. They also stock chemicals for water quality maintenance in hot tubs and spas. Al's is a great source for top of the line patio and outdoor furniture like the Tropitone, and director chairs by Telescope, which look as good inside as out. For your recreation room or home bar, there's a complete line of card tables and chairs, plus fine Samsonite bar stools. Any budget, any season, easy livin' is the trade at Al's.
Visa. Master Charge.

The Foam Shop

5311 ROOSEVELT WAY N.E.
525-2301
HOURS: MONDAY-
SATURDAY 10:00-6:00
SUNDAY 12-5:00

A place to buy a piece of foam to sleep or sit on is something everyone needs at one time or another. So it makes sense to tell you about an especially good foam place, The Foam Shop in the University District. They carry foam in every different density, firmness, shape and size, covering every possible use . . . mattresses, living room furniture, pillows, instrument cases for cameras and sound equipment, boat cushions and backpacking

equipment. The Foam Shop people are very good at explaining the logic behind the correct choice of foam for your project. You'll also find many ideas and patterns for constructing beds, furniture and accessories, along with fabric, frames and other materials you'll need.

If you've decided to save money and do your own redecorating, you might as well do it right! Visa. Master Charge.

Fuzzy Wuzzy Rug Company

815 EAST LAKE AVENUE E.
623-2957
HOURS: MONDAY-FRIDAY 8:00-5:00
SATURDAY 9:00 AM-12 NOON

Fuzzy Wuzzy Rug Company is the oldest and most respected carpet cleaning business in Seattle. It was started in 1900 by Joseph Ellison, an English rug weaver. He was joined in 1906 by the Beymer family who have the rug company ever since. They have been operating from their Eastlake plant since 1947, providing great service in both rug and upholstery cleaning. Many people wouldn't consider going anywhere else, particularly for cleaning of antique furniture and rugs. Fuzzy Wuzzy is also known for their amazing results with

water-damaged items, but have complete facilities for the more routine binding, serging, fringing and new seaming tasks. The service includes free pick-up and delivery of furniture and loose rugs, or if you prefer, the cleaning may be done in your own home with the finest portable equipment. If you have what you think is an insoluble problem, just call them. Chances are they've seen it before and can solve it in no time.
Visa. Master Charge.

Don Willis Unfinished Furniture

10516 LAKE CITY WAY N.E.
524-9944
HOURS: MONDAY-THURSDAY 9:30-7:00
FRIDAY UNTIL 8:30
SATURDAY UNTIL 5:30
SUNDAY 12:30-4:30

Don Willis Unfinished Furniture is the largest and most reputable unfinished furniture outlet in Seattle. The same family has run the business since it opened 30 years ago, and they take a real pride in their credibility. This is actually more like a warehouse than a retail store, with 3 floors of furniture of all kinds and styles . . . bookcases, antique reproductions, outdoor furniture, stereo cabinets, baby furniture, mirrors, butcher block tables, beds and chairs. One could go on and on as the selection indeed does. You'll find a good variety of both soft and hard woods and one of the best collections of solid oak anywhere. Everything is unfinished so prices are extremely affordable. Don Willis also carries all the finishing supplies you'll need, and staff will spend as much time with you as it takes to demonstrate simple finishing techniques. A prompt delivery service is also offered, to bring your purchase right to your doorstep.
Visa. Master Charge.

Rumpelstiltskin

NORTHGATE MALL 365-0400
SOUTHCENTER MALL 246-8750
CAPITOL HILL: 112A BROADWAY AVENUE E.
    329-8750
BELLEVUE: 421 BELLEVUE WAY N.E.
    453-8720
BELLINGHAM: 1205 CORNWALL
    734-8750
OLYMPIA: CAPITAL MALL 754-8770
ALDERWOOD MALL: 771-3868

That little man in the fairy tale had a hard act to follow with his straw-into-gold routine, but you can come pretty close to that at Rumpelstiltskin. They

have all the fabric and accessories with which to work your own home decorating miracles . . . or, if you're not quite ready to tackle a project with confidence, they conduct classes in every kind of needlecraft from trapunto to cross-stitching and back again. But if you're more like Sleeping Beauty — all thumbs when it comes to a thimble — Rumpelstiltskin offers many custom design services. Tell them what you want and they'll create pillows, quilts, window curtains, knit clothing and fabric wall hangings. In either case, you may select from the astonishing variety of quality yardage, yarn, needlecraft supplies, fabric wall panels, trimmings, ribbons, belting, buttons, buckles, flounces and froo-fraws. A visit to Rumpelstiltskin generates a rush of ideas, and it's hard to leave without a yard of this, a snippet of that, and some silver thread, just in case.
Visa. Master Charge. TransAction.

Specialties

Photo: Historical Society of Seattle & King County

You mean people actually live here!

Southside Johnny of Southside Johnny and the Asbury Jukes

Eastern Onion

Singing Telegram Service

1471 130TH AVENUE N.E.
BELLEVUE
453-1212
OFFICE HOURS: MONDAY-FRIDAY 9:30-5:30
SATURDAY 10:00-3:00
RECORDING SERVICE DURING EVENING
HOURS.

Eastern Onion has brought back the singing telegram, which in some people's minds, ranks as one of the great achievements of the 20th Century. In an age that takes itself too seriously, Eastern Onion is refreshing. There are more than 45 different messages in their repertoire, including the usual Happy Birthdays (and a few unusual ones), Mother's Day greetings, Welcome Home . . . to more esoteric requirements like Bill Collection, as well as a few involving Superman or Wonder Woman. Eastern Onion messengers take their assignments *very* seriously. They'll arrive clad in top hat, pink chemise and red tuxedo after slogging through rain, hail, sleet, snow or dark of night to deliver whatever to whomever, wherever you choose. They also pack a mechanical monkey and kazoo, or maybe the Singing Birthday Cake, because they don't believe in doing things halfway. It's got to be the best way to dazzle someone who has everything else, and it's available in 25 cities. Seattle Onions Walt Sweger, Robert Johnson and Tonya Johnson can usually arrange local deliveries with 24 hours notice. Come on, try it once. You'll get hooked.
Visa. Master Charge.

custom stationery and invitations

William Ernest Brown

**1333 - 5TH AVENUE
RAINIER SQUARE
292-9404
HOURS: MONDAY-SATURDAY 10:00-5:30
10630 N.E. 8TH AVENUE
GELATI PLACE
BELLEVUE
455-3665
HOURS: MONDAY-SATURDAY 10:00-5:00**

Take it from a writer: there's just nothing quite like the pleasure of writing on beautiful paper, and there's no writing paper in Seattle to compare with the selection at William Ernest Brown. This is the kind of place that used to be called a stationery store, but is really much more. Small, well-appointed and elegant, William Ernest Brown is the city's most complete source for custom social stationery. They also have invitations, announcements of all kinds, desk accessories and party accoutrements that feature the finest names in writing products, like G. Lalo of France, Fante, Mary Quant and Crane. Designs range from whimsical and witty to elegant handmade creations; all bearing taste and imagination. Owners Sue Silberman and Connie Brown particularly welcome special projects. They'll arrange for desk accessories to match your personal decor or create custom-made invitations and announcements which may even be addressed and mailed on your behalf. There are designers and calligraphers on call at William Ernest Brown to lend a unique flourish to your social impression.

James Crosby

2832 - 80TH AVENUE S.E.
MERCER ISLAND, WN. 98040
232-3714
HOURS: MONDAY-SATURDAY 10:00-5:30
WEEKDAY EVENINGS IN DECEMBER

No, James Crosby is not the Mayor of Mercer Island, but he *is* a problem solver, and his shop has made the Island a destination point for gift hunters. The Island Crest Way exit off I-90 leads you to a cozy old home in the business district, where James himself used to live. Now it's filled with unusual and useful gifts, and it's completely relaxing because you know you'll find something in all those many rooms for that impossible person who seems to have everything already. You'll discover a complete line of dinnerware by Heath Stoneware, Hadley, and El Palomar, Pfalzgraf and others, plus Boda crystal, stationery, linens, cards, candles, kitchen items, bath products, imported rugs and jewelry. From contemporary design products to whimsical miniatures, James Crosby has them. And if you need something so special or obscure that you've almost abandoned hope, ask at James Crosby. Word has it that he just can't resist the challenge. Next door is his women's wear shop, featuring classic separates and accessories in mostly natural fabrics, from Jones of New York, John Meyer, Breckenridge, and others. James Crosby offers worldwide shipping and local delivery services, as well as a bridal registry. Christmas is a special time to visit, with two rooms entirely devoted to holiday items and decorations. The conveniences of a large department store, and the personal touch of James Crosby make shopping here a pleasure.
Visa. Master Charge.

Crissey's
Flowers and Gifts

RAINIER SQUARE - 5TH & UNIVERSITY
624-6661

2100 - 5TH AVENUE AT LENORA
622-1100

HOURS: MONDAY-SATURDAY 8:30-5:30

Crissey's will expand your impression of what a flower shop or gift shop should be. There are so many things here that you've never seen before, it's more like a living, blooming museum. From sculptured clay pots to bronzed garden faucets, variety and innovation are the marks of distinction here. There is an emphasis on quality and many items are exclusive, to be found at Crissey's alone. It's fertile ground for new ideas and sincere thought. If you stop in to buy a spontaneous rose for someone who least expects it, don't be surprised if you're inspired to give a silk orchid arranged with pheasant feathers instead. Because nothing is a half-thought at Crissey's, the vase will be as attractive as the blossom, the card as artful as the gift. For over 30 years James Chrissey has integrated the floral life of this city with the artistic and cultural life. Each season is a celebration, each celebration is a fresh endeavor. There are no repeats and no formulas when designing arrangements and decor for special occasions. Because of this attention, a great deal of personalized work is done here. You can bring in containers or samples of a color scheme and arrangements will be created to complement. Many customers are so familiar they need only call and say "entry hall." At Crissey's you'll find the intrigue of a museum and the attention of a salon, plus flowers, gifts and holiday decor.

Visa. Master Charge. American Express. Carte Blanche.

T & N

1220 - 1ST AVENUE
622-0516
HOURS: MONDAY-SATURDAY 10:00-6:00
SUNDAY 12-4:00

Tony and Nina Ventura are celebrated in Seattle for their beautiful clothing designs, but they haven't always been terribly easy to find. That situation has been remedied, however, by the opening of their new retail store, T & N. The shop features not only their own skillfully made, highly original creations for men and women, but an interesting selection of Chinese antique furniture and other clothing as well. During a stint in Paris, Tony and Nina became enamoured of the strong Chinese influence there and came home to contribute their knowledge to exhibitions of Eastern textiles and art here in Seattle . . . notably at the Wing Luke Museum. But that was just a warm-up act for T & N. They have now gathered together contemporary clothing from China, other special well-priced clothing finds, Chinese folk art and furniture, altar tables, temple carvings, antique textiles, silver jewelry, embroidered shawls and even 20th century children's puppets. T & N has become the perfect reflection of the varied tastes and sensibilities of Tony and Nina. That's what makes it so special. Visa. Master Charge.

Etal

421 CEDAR STREET
292-9300
HOURS: TUESDAY-SATURDAY 11:00-5:30

The first things one notices about Etal are the calm, uncluttered decor and the absolutely arresting color of the walls. The next thing one realizes is that it is either a very beautifully decorated flower store or a very fragrant gift shop. Actually, it is both. Etal has a collection of innovative gifts and decorative accessories for the home or office, ranging from elegant vases to unusual writing paper, gathered from Italy, Paris, New York and all over the world. You'll find good taste and style in the inexpensive as well as the elegant . . . basketry, brass, fine porcelain and glassware. Located in the same store is Etal's custom floral design service, providing floral arrangements for your home or the final touch on special occasions. In fact, Etal may be the only place in town where you'll find the perfect vase and the perfect rose to go in it.
Visa. Master Charge. American Express.

Off Broadway

207 HARVARD AVENUE E.
324-6966
HOURS: MONDAY-FRIDAY 10:00-5:30
SATURDAY 11:00-5:00 OR BY APPT.

Off Broadway is a real find. It's one of those one-of-a-kind stores that make living in the city a pleasure. Located on Capitol Hill, just off Broadway, it's a bed-and-bath store that isn't just a bed and bath store. For starters, they specialize in custom-designing down comforters to your specifications. You can choose from a myriad of tasteful patterns, fabrics, sizes and quilting styles. Only the finest European white goose down is used, and if you prefer, Off Broadway will stitch up a fiberfill comforter for the warmer months. Then there are custom-made bed accessories, monogrammed cotton sheets, and a complete line of towels and other designer bath furnishings. But the touch that makes Off Broadway unique is the lovely sleepwear and lingerie from Christian Dior, Bill Tice, and Geoffrey Beene . . . the perfect finishing touch to a truly sybaritic store. Visa. Master Charge.

Creme Soda

203 - 1ST AVENUE S.
62-CREME
HOURS: MONDAY-SUNDAY 12:00-5:30
FRIDAY & SATURDAY NIGHTS 8:30-11:30

Creme Soda gives brand new meaning to the 1930's expression, "flaming youth." Specializing in tasteful sleaze, this outrageous little shop in Pioneer Square carries the best of both the past and the present. Old toys, 1930's hand-painted ties, Hawaiian shirts and lingerie with lots of razz-ma-tazz mix freely with the newest, most on-the-edge, outlandish creations for scene-stealers and scene-makers of all ages. This place defies classification because the stuff runs from soup to nuts, but just to mention a few things, consider this: notecards with fabulous illustrations and lots of room for a shocking declaration of passion or a well-chosen insult, coffee mugs shaped like penguins and ducks, or shirts and ties, beaded belts, cashmere sweaters, old kimonos, clear plastic neckties you can fill up with goldfish, pins with superheroes, sexy pin-ups, rhinestone stars, kissing lips or snappy sayings — in short, all those things your mother never used to let you buy. Next time you want to cause a stir, you'll find all the equipment you need at Creme Soda, home of the classiest neon sign in Seattle.
Visa. Master Charge.

Pike Place Flowers

**1ST & PIKE,
PIKE PLACE MARKET
682-9799
5TH & PINE ST.,
FREDERICK &
NELSON
382-8221
HOURS: MONDAY-
SATURDAY 9:30-5:30**

The corner of First and Pike has never looked so bloomin' beautiful thanks to Pike Place Flowers. This charming outdoor shop is a fountain of bouquets, baskets, greenery, and blossoming plants adorning the corner sidewalk of the market. A dedicated staff of flower lovers have helped to establish this shop, a result of owner Drake Salladay's desire to offer all the things he had never been able to find in Seattle. And now, Pike Place Flowers has blossomed in a second location. It's on the first floor of Frederick & Nelson at 5th and Pine. On a typical day at Pike Place Flowers, you'll see a lush gathering of field grown and hothouse flowers from or for every climate. Many of the selections are available pre-season. In the drab of winter you can still bring home fressia, runsunculus, iris, daisies, tiger lilies, and exotic protea from Australia. Dried flowers are in fine form here . . . lots and lots of them, artfully arranged in baskets from many foreign markets. At the F & N location, Pike Place Flowers offers floral designs to order for all occasions. They accept requests to locate flowers not carried, and will dispatch arrangements by cab right to your door.
Visa. Master Charge. Frederick & Nelson at F & N.

Mr. Peepers

2665 N. VILLAGE MALL
UNIVERSITY VILLAGE
SEATTLE, WASHINGTON 98105
(206) 522-8202
HOURS: MONDAY-SATURDAY 10:00-6:00
THURSDAY AND FRIDAY UNTIL 9:00
OPEN SUNDAYS 12-5:00 FROM
THANKSGIVING TO CHRISTMAS

Mr. Peepers enjoys national acclaim as one of the best miniatures shops in the country, but knowing that doesn't begin to cover what this shop is all about. In fact, it's very hard to say what you'll find when you visit. Hobby miniaturists know Mr. Peepers as the place to furnish the definitive dollhouse, but other people like the wonderful toys, stuffed animals, wood carvings, pyramids, nutcrackers, music boxes, Russian lacquer boxes and lots of intriquing handmade articles by Northwest artisans of all disciplines. Expect the unexpected, and you'll still be surprised, because Mr. Peepers does something totally different for every major season, holiday and celebration. The 1979 Christmas theme, for example, centers on the newly acquired 1928 mint ragtop Model A Ford truck. It's in working condition but it's not going anywhere because it will be chockfull of Mr. Peepers' collection of ornaments, decorations and gifts. All the items are hand-picked by owners Allan Davis and Barbara Raftery from over 600 sources, and cover a price range of 50¢ to $20,000. All in all, Mr. Peepers has cornered the market on the original, unusual and charming.
Visa. Master Charge.

Great Things

426 BROADWAY AVENUE E.
325-3200
HOURS: MONDAY-SATURDAY
11:00-5:30

If you needed to find the perfect gift and only had time to visit one store, your best bet would be Great Things on Broadway. There are people who do their entire Christmas list here without missing a beat.

This store is filled with great things that run the gamut from tastefully elegant to terribly outrageous. Much of the stock falls into the category of accessories for the home, but Great Things also carries stationery from Fante and other well-known manufacturers, posters, baskets, soft sculpture, candles, art glass and lots of unique, unusual and one-of-a-kind gifts. The crystal department is especially fine with exquisite vases, paperweights, candle-holders, and glassware. The card selection is regarded as one of the most entertaining in Seattle — if you want a greeting or illustration that will knock 'em dead, look here first.
Visa. Master Charge. American Express.

sense, but rendered from the special European pottery process); hand-sheared, full-lead crystal including everyday stemware and limited edition pieces; originally crafted pewter plates; handpainted Limoges china dishes and picture frames; silk flowers, candleholders and distinctive baskets. Even delightful indulgences like the French Faience rabbits, sheep, goat and geese hold true as genuine additions to a European provincial decor theme. There are unexpected touches, too . . . a gift shopper who has an executive-with-everything in mind might appreciate opening an exquisite leather attache to find an elaborate toy train. You'll encounter a similar flair for imagination throughout the store. The gift registry, for example, allows the expression of general preferences rather than just one pattern. The owner feels that there are no aesthetic limitations to practicality, and that shopping for specialty pieces should be intriguing and enjoyable. Those who agree will find that E.M. Wilkinson, in the serenity of Rainier Square, will stimulate and satisfy those sensibilities.
Visa. Master Charge.

E.M. Wilkinson

RAINIER SQUARE ATRIUM
FIFTH AVENUE
623-6233
HOURS: MONDAY-SATURDAY 10:00-5:30

E.M. Wilkinson is a store like no other in the city. The space is filled with select decorator and personal gifts that anyone with a refined taste will instantly admire. But a closer look reveals that a specific theme unifies this taste. The owner has chosen each object according to a seasoned preference for country elegance in the French style. The collection here is emphatic testimony that purely decorative items are as important to an environment as the gracefully functional ones you'll find in the store. The displays are arrestingly beautiful . . . large antique armoires hold things like Faience dishware (not manufactured in the usual

Folk Art Gallery/ La Tienda

4138 UNIVERSITY WAY N.E.
UNIVERSITY DISTRICT
632-1796
HOURS: TUESDAY-SATURDAY 10:00-5:30
THURSDAY UNTIL 9:00

Folk Art Gallery, formerly known as La Tienda, is one of Seattle's best known shops for many reasons. First, they do some of the most intriguing windows in town. It's hard to pass by without being drawn in by some remarkable treasure from an exotic corner of the globe. Which leads to another reason why this place has had a city-wide attraction for over 15 years . . . the selection. Owner Leslie Hart travels all over the world to bring under one roof the many beautiful, unusual and frequently museum-quality folk arts and textiles; a fact that has been noted by The New York Times. This selection covers all price ranges and categories: jewelry, toys, clothing, notecards, wall-hangings, utensils, musical instruments and furniture. There's also a unique selection of books related to ethnographic material and folk art of the world.
Visa. Master Charge. American Express.

Barnier's Town & Country Pet Store

1314 - 1ST AVENUE
622-9093

Barnier's Town & Country Pet Store has been awarding diplomas to some of Seattle's wittiest and most literate feathered friends for 60 years. Founded in 1918 by the late Mrs. J. L. Barnier, wife of a well-known Seattle veterinarian, this shop actually houses a bird school where professionals will tame your birds or teach them to talk. Barnier's also has developed its own mix of bird seed, and they can custom-mix the best diet for almost any breed. The bird hospital at Barnier's has an excellent and experienced staff and they offer vacation boarding facilities as well. Barnier's carries a complete supply of accessories for all kinds of other pets, too. And, of course, no visit to the shop is complete without stopping to exchange a few quips with Robert, Barnier's famous talking mynah bird, who will probably remind you of someone you know.
Visa. Master Charge.

Seattle Art Museum: The Museum Stores

SEATTLE ART MUSEUM AT VOLUNTEER PARK ON CAPITOL HILL
447-4710
HOURS: TUESDAY-SATURDAY
10:00 A.M.-5:00 P.M.
TUESDAY & THURSDAY EVENING
7:00 P.M.-10:00 P.M.
SUNDAY 12:00 NOON-5:00 P.M.
CLOSED MONDAYS

SEATTLE ART MUSEUM, MODERN ART PAVILLION AT SEATTLE CENTER
447-4795
HOURS: TUESDAY-SUNDAY
11:00 A.M.-6:00 P.M.
THURSDAY EVENING 6:00 P.M.-8:00 P.M.
CLOSED MONDAYS

In Europe, museum shopping is very popular. Well, you can do it in Seattle, too. The Seattle Art Museum has shops in both of its locations: the Modern Art Pavillion at the Seattle Center and at Volunteer Park on Capitol Hill. Both shops have a fine selection of gifts, jewelry, books, posters, prints and stationery. Many of the items are finely-made museum reproductions of the exhibited objects. The Museum is proud of its collection of art books, and you can often find limited publications of books and catalogs featuring many local and national artists. There are always posters available from current museum shows, as well as editions from past shows. Other paper products run the gamut from children's project-books and stories, to notecards and postcards. The price range is exceptionally good. Printing quality and reproduction are always fine-grade, and many items may be special-ordered. The Seattle Art Museum stores are great places to find unusual, beautiful (and even inexpensive) gifts to please almost anyone.
Visa. Master Charge.

Seattle
Tent & Fabric

MARINERS SQUARE
1900 N. NORTHLAKE WAY
632-6022
HOURS: MONDAY-FRIDAY 10:00-6:00
SATURDAY 10:00-4:00

Seattle Tent & Fabric has been around since 1897, when its main occupation was making circus tents. In its present incarnation, it is a recreational fabric store, specializing in do-it-yourself projects as well as custom-sewing for an almost limitless range of needs. The Mariners Square location, however, gives a clue to its chief focus, and that is of course, nautical equipment. Seattle Tent & Fabric turns out sail boat covers, duffel bags, tote bags, other custom-made items for all kinds of boats as well as cushion repair, draperies and Roman shades. If you are intending to do it yourself, you'll find a range of instructional material for many marine-related accessories. The selection of acrylic, nylon and canvas fabrics come in a wide variety of widths, weights and colors that can be done up into banners, baby backpacks, directors chairs, pillows, awnings, and of course, tents of any size. Free sewing seminars are held monthly; each one concentrating on a particular project. If you attend and flunk the course, don't worry because Seattle Tent & Fabric staff are all sewing experts who can make your project to order.
Visa. Master Charge.

Bergman Luggage

DOWNTOWN SEATTLE
2122 - 3RD AVENUE
622-2354
BELLEVUE/REDMOND
15116 N.E. 24TH STREET
643-2344
FEDERAL WAY
CENTER PLAZA
ACROSS FROM SEA/TAC MALL
2012 S. 320TH STREET
941-7990

Bergman's is the last word in fine luggage in Seattle. They've been in business for 52 years now, carrying virtually every major brand. Their key to success isn't complicated: the finest quality products in huge quantities at prices you won't find anywhere else. The owners are Simon and Geraldine Hurwitz, and son Jay, who is in charge of the expansion program. The Hurwitz family is famous for their genuine concern about service. They employ a close-knit staff who serve their customers well, many of whom have been with the company for many years and know the merchandise inside out. The selection is outstanding and includes trunks, suitcases, attaches, handbags, wallets and fine accessories from the world's leading manufacturers . . . Lark, Ventura, Samsonite, American Tourister, Skyway, Renwick of Canada, Wings, Bond Street, Prince Gardner, Halliburton and St. Thomas; also fine Italian imports. Bergman's luggage repair service is used by all the major airlines as their Seattle replacement and repair depot for lost or damaged items. For a personal touch on your new luggage and leather items, their shop does gold-leaf monogramming. The recently-opened, beautifully designed Bellevue and Federal Way stores are a sight to behold; quality merchandise, beautifully displayed. The homey, no-nonsense downtown store is truly a store to explore; masses of merchandise piled high. Si Hurwitz likes it that way, and observes with humor that the new stores come complete with new people (and so young yet), since after so many years, the 3rd Avenue staff couldn't bear to leave the original Bergman's. You can count on the same attention to service and fine selection at each of their three stores.
Master Charge. BankAmericard.

 # Burback & Bollinger's Funtastic Traveling Show

**WESTERN WASHINGTON FAIR
ASSOCIATION
PUYALLUP, WASHINGTON
PLEASE CALL 1-695-8094
FOR INFORMATION**

Come one, come all — to the most exciting show on earth . . . the Burback & Bollinger Funtastic Traveling Show! Together Robert Bollinger and Ron Burback present one of the most respected carnivals in North America, and one of the largest. Mr.

Bollinger's father started the ball rolling way back in 1905. He sold popcorn at Portland's Oaks Park Amusement Center, bought one ride, which led to another and then another. Robert joined the business some years ago, and today he and Ron Burback offer about 130 rides and one hundred games of skill. But theirs is no ordinary carnival. The games policy is liberal (which means lots of winners), and the crew is decked out in uniform or snappy white shirt and tie. Add to that a genuine love of good old-fashioned laughter, thrills and entertainment, and the sum is the best carnival around. Leading all this fun is the absolutely astounding and undeniably lovable Captain Funtastic, irresistable to kids and adults alike. Burback and Bollinger's Funtastic Traveling Show is a large operation, set up to play everything from the biggest fairs to the littlest shopping centers; you can rent the whole show or just one merry-go-round. So come one, come all . . . and have a ball!

Innervisions

4214 UNIVERSITY WAY N.E.
634-2392
HOURS: MONDAY-
SATURDAY 10:00-6:00
THURSDAY UNTIL 9:00
SUNDAY 12-5:00

Collecting and appreciating posters is an avocation that has been practised for years, and Innervisions does that tradition proud. Innervisions specializes in advertising posters, prints, old fruit crate labels, film posters, album covers, museum posters and New York theatre posters. The shop is owned by Steve Delph, who's been a fan of this particular art form for years and is in touch with sources for it from all over the country and the world. Along with familiar names like David Lance Goines, Patrick Nagel and Loren Salazar, you'll also find a more esoteric selection that includes everything from Museum of Modern Art productions to Rainier beer posters, as well as pieces commissioned for local festivities like Bumbershoot, Fat Tuesday and various theatre and dance events. Innervisions also provides a complete custom or do-it-yourself framing service, with all the supplies you'll need. If you've been looking for a hard-to-find item, ask them about it, since they can special-order almost anything.

Visa. Master Charge.

Douglas-Harris Ltd. of England

1525 - 6TH AVENUE
PLEASE CHECK LOCAL TELEPHONE
LISTING.
HOURS: MONDAY-SATURDAY 9:00-6:00

Douglas Harris is a newcomer to Seattle, but its origin goes back to 1966 when Marc Alport made his first trip to the British Isles. It was the beginning of a 23-year love affair culminating in the creation of a store devoted to bringing the finest in British merchandise to the Pacific Northwest. Marc and partner Craig Dewey have the combined experience of nearly 20 years in the British marketplace, and Douglas-Harris has formed ties with literally hundreds of British firms. The Company's good standing in England has enabled development of working relationships with many small, unknown firms that have previously avoided the American market. At Douglas-Harris you'll find the best of Scotland, Wales and England, with the finest in men's, women's and children's British fashions. There are accessories like cosmetics, perfumes, gourmet foods, luggage, books and handmade toys, and an English lambskin coat collection that is second to none. Douglas-Harris can fit men in sizes small to extra large, as well as shorts, regulars and longs in suits and sport coats. Women's sizes are six to eighteen. The selection is superb, the service refreshingly knowlegeable and, in some cases, unique to Seattle: like arrangements for shooting lessons with London's most renowned gunmaker, Holland & Holland.

Visa. Master Charge. American Express.

M. J. Feet

Birkenstock Footwear

4334 UNIVERSITY WAY N.E.
632-5353
HOURS: MONDAY-FRIDAY 10:00-7:00
THURSDAY UNTIL 9:00
SATURDAY 10:00-6:00

MJ Feet doesn't look like other shoe stores. First of all, the inside is warm and round and comforting, with bright colors on the walls. Secondly, it has evolved over the years from a shoe store into a place where you can find such unusual items as silk underwear, cotton umbrellas, natural fiber socks, and who knows what other surprises. Owners Melanie and Charles Grimes pride themselves on giving their clientele personal attention, so they'll get the best possible fit and feel. MJ Feet has a complete line of Birkenstock shoes, which were invented 205 years ago, to provide maximum arch support and comfort. The design has prevailed and these shoes are still popular the world over. If you're looking for shoes that feel good then you've come to the right place. And what other shoe store allows you to walk out with a great pair of shoes for your feet and an umbrella for your head as well? Only MJ Feet.
Master Charge. BankAmericard.

Nordic House

218 1ST AVENUE SOUTH
GRAND CENTRAL ON THE PARK
682-5684
HOURS: MONDAY-SATURDAY 10:00-5:00
SUNDAY 12-5:00

Nordic means "north", but to many people, it also means the very best in modern design. Nordic House, in the Grand Central Building at Pioneer Square, is the perfect example of that concept. Manager Britta Bergman specializes in gifts and clothing that reflect the clean lines and functional designs that nordic countries are famous for. There are sleek "iittala" crystal and woolen blankets from Finland; Hadeland tableware as well as ethnic sweaters, mittens, caps, gloves and stockings from Norway; Swedish pewter jewelry, clogs, crystal and fine linens; and of course, incomparable Royal Copenhagen porcelain from Denmark. The Nordic House also features the Northwest's largest selection of amber jewelry, which is made from "fossilized" resin from prehistoric conifer trees. Whether you're looking for the most elegant modern dinnerware, collector's plates or some snazzy socks to keep you warm and authentic-looking on the cross country trails, the Nordic House is the place to start looking.
Visa. Master Charge. TransAction.

The Scottish Shopper

**14202 - 1ST AVENUE S.
SEATTLE, WASHINGTON 98168
(206) 242-1768, (206) 242-0291
HOURS: TUESDAY-SATURDAY 9:30-5:30**

You couldn't find a better selection of beautiful wool clothing and Tartan fabrics than you'll see at The Scottish Shopper, unless you dashed off to Edinburgh for the weekend. Assuming that's out of

the question, The Scottish Shopper is the next best thing. They have wool Tartan/plaid yardage and garments, warm wool knitwear, records, books, pottery, glassware and plaques . . . all emblazoned with authentic Scottish clan crests. All are imported from Scotland, of course; bearing the best brand names in the realm, like Barrie Knitwear, Andrew Stewart, Locharron, Robert Mackie, R.G. Lawrie, Carrick and Ortak. Their Tartan fabric has even been to the moon in the hands of astronaut Allan Bean, making history on its own. And, by the way, if you have a musical turn, The Scottish Shopper carries bagpipes and all related items, too. Now there's something that will please the neighbors! Visa. Master Charge.

 # Seattle Knife Supply

1916 PIKE PLACE
682-4563
HOURS: MONDAY-SATURDAY 9:00-6:00

Seattle Knife Supply, located in Pike Place Market, is a virtual department store for cutting tools of every description. This is where to come if you need the right bladed implement for a special job. You'll find kitchen knives, hunting and pocket knives, heavy duty scissors, sewing scissors and shears, woodcarving and gardening implements, beautiful steak knife sets and carving blades. Seattle Knife Supply stocks only top-drawer brand names and lots of them, all bearing the kind of superior craftsmanship you can depend on to get the job done with precision. Also a full-service sharpening and repair center, Seattle Knife Supply is the home of the city's cutting edge.

Warshal's Sporting Goods

**1000 - 1ST AVENUE
LOCATED HALFWAY
BETWEEN PIKE PLACE
MARKET AND PIONEER
SQUARE
624-7300
HOURS: MONDAY-
SATURDAY 9:00-5:30
FRIDAY UNTIL 9:00**

Every good photographer in town knows that one of the best places to go for complete photographic and darkroom supplies is Warshal's Sporting Goods. Cohabitating with all the hunting and fishing merchandise, athletic gear and outdoor clothing, the camera department is really a store in its own right. All major lines of camera equipment are available, including Cambo, Nikon, Canon, Pentax, Minolta, Fujica, Konica, Eumig, Mamiya, Bell & Howell, Vivitar and many, many more. Cameras and lenses of all sizes are stocked, including equipment for 4x5 and 5x7 formats. Since Warshal's is a major source for much of the commercial photography that takes place in Seattle, it's a good place to check if you're looking for used equipment as well. There is also,

of course, everything in the way of darkroom supplies; indeed the largest open supply of papers, chemicals and film in the area. Photographic lighting equipment, tripods, enlargers and books on the subject are available, too . . . in short, everything to take you from capturing the image to displaying the finished print. Staff make a point of becoming familiar with photographers' needs and gear their stock to anticipate upcoming purchases. Prices are usually a little lower than the same products at other outlets . . . another reason why both professional and amateur photographers have depended on Warshal's photography department since 1936. That's quite a record.

All major bank cards. House Accounts.

 # Grand Prix Motors

1401 12TH AVENUE
329-7070
HOURS: MONDAY-FRIDAY 8:00-6:00
SATURDAY 10:00-5:00

When you think of the high life, you think of fast, sleek, elegant automobiles, and when you think of that, Grand Prix Motors comes immediately to mind. That's where you'll find Seattle's finest stable of Ferraris, straight from Italy. Grand Prix Motors chooses the Ferrari for its exhilarating design, excellent craftsmanship, and superb road handling and response . . . the qualities of a great high performance luxury car. One of the top automobile dealers in the nation, Grand Prix Motors has created a strong Ferrari market in Seattle through its reputation for first-class service and maintenance departments. Aware that a Ferrari owner takes his driving experience seriously, they place much emphasis on providing individual attention to every customer and his needs. When you're ready for your Ferrari, visit Grand Prix Motors . . . they'll be ready for you.

University Porsche/Audi

4724 ROOSEVELT WAY N.E.
(206) 634-3322
Telex: 32-8888
HOURS:
SALES: MONDAY-FRIDAY 8:00-8:00
SATURDAY 10:00-5:00
SERVICE & PARTS: MONDAY-FRIDAY
7:00-6:00
PARTS ONLY: SATURDAY 10:00-4:00

Most people will never own an Aston-Martin or top-of-the-line Porsche, but those who do find that there's no better place to drive one than in Seattle, because people come from all over the country to have theirs serviced at University Porsche/Audi. This dealership has developed its leading reputation by cultivating a staff of mechanics and salespeople who are thoroughly trained in the kind of service and attention required to keep these high-performance automobiles in peak condition. The selection of Aston-Martin and Porsche models is one of the nation's very best, a distinction that has won University Porsche/Audi many awards. In fact, they serve as a Product Quality Monitor for the factory, road-testing models up to a year before they go on the market. Even if you're not buying a car, University Porsche/Audi is worth a visit to inspect the accessories shop, with its unique array of Porsche ''signature'' fashions, jewelry, books, racing gear and car care products; many of them custom-made for these luxury automobiles and the people who own them . . . or wish they did.
Visa. Master Charge. Standard Oil cards.

Silver Fox
Limousine Service

622-2709
14527 N.E. 40TH
BELLEVUE, WA. 98007

Let's face it — when it comes to flat out class, nothing beats a chauffeured limousine. And there's no classier limo service than the Silver Fox. Just because VIPs like Kris Kristofferson and Evel Knievel regularly use Silver Fox doesn't mean you should be shy about it. Step right up and do it — you deserve it and everyone can afford it. A telephone call will have your Silver Fox chauffeur arriving at the appointed hour in a sleek black Cadillac that will knock your socks off. All *you* do is sit back and relax in its plush comfort, with television and wet bar at your service, while you're whisked off to the concert, soire, basketball game, hot tub parlor or diplomatic reception. What an entrance! What a great birthday idea! Or way to show visiting business associates that extra consideration. When you think of all the marvelous experiences you'd like but never have, a chauffeured limo presents itself as very possible indeed; you have to try it once. Whoever you'd like to impress, whatever the destination, every occasion can't help but be even more special when the Silver Fox is in charge of getting you there.

Marine Specialties

Photo: Historical Society of Seattle & King County

*If you could only get the Columbia River to flow through Los Angeles county,
you could give Detroit and Pittsburg back to the Indians.*

"San Francisco Chronicle"

Vic Franck's Boat Company

1109 N. NORTHLAKE WAY
632-7000

Vic and Dan Franck are grand masters at their trade ...building boats. For many who have waited half a lifetime to take to the sea, that means building dreams, and those dreams can be trusted with this company. Established in 1927, it's one of the oldest custom boat design companies in the area, and unquestionably one of the best. All aspects of boat construction are undertaken in-house, including machining, painting, carpentry, upholstery and finishing work. Vic Franck's staff of skilled and experienced craftsmen have much to do with the company's worldwide reputation for innovative design and a unique application of traditional methods. They do all their own design and engineering work as well, and pioneered one of the first turbine-powered pleasure boats in the country. All-important maintenance work is also undertaken; rebuilding, remodeling and repair of new and old boats accounts for nearly half of their business. Some of the sleekest seagoing vessels in Seattle have been placed in their care, and every one of them comes back shipshape and seaworthy.

Crow's Nest

SUITE 155, MARINERS SQUARE
1900 N. NORTHLAKE WAY
632-3555
HOURS: MONDAY-SATURDAY 9:00-6:00

6010 SEAVIEW AVENUE N.W.
783-6262
HOURS: MONDAY-SATURDAY 8:30-6:00
SUNDAY 9:00-4:00

The Crow's Nest is one of the city's foremost marine supply sources. If it's top quality and goes on a boat, it's here. Opened in 1971, The Crow's Nest is a thriving offshoot of the Fisheries Supply Company, itself an intriguing chunk of Seattle seafaring history. It was started 51 years ago by the Sutter family as a service which put together everything for the commercial fisherman. And in the old days, that included groceries delivered right to the boat. The Crow's Nest shows the benefits of that experience everywhere you turn through the comprehensive array of sailing, yachting, rafting and power boat accessories. Barient Winches, Avon inflatable boats, Woolsey marine paint, Wilcox-Crittendon hardware are some of the essential items they carry, and anything you need and don't see may be special-ordered. If you're a strictly dry-land sailor and like to read, there is a good stock of marine books. You'll find the Crow's Nest has maintained the friendliness and concern for each customer that has been the hallmark of the Sutter family business in Seattle.
Visa. Master Charge.

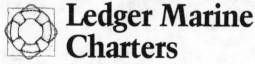 # Ledger Marine Charters

101 NICKERSON, SUITE 200
283-6160
HOURS: MONDAY-FRIDAY 9:00-5:00
SATURDAY 10:00-4:00

There are over 3,000 miles of unexcelled, protected cruising waters from Seattle to Alaska, so Ledger Marine Charters invites you to enjoy some of the world's best cruising. You may charter U-Drive boats, both power and sail, ranging in size from 26 to 55 feet long. The larger, luxurious yachts range in size from 50 to 126 feet, and are chartered with complete crew. If you are arranging a charter for an organized group, Ledger Marine has a number of Coast Guard Licensed Passenger Vessels which can accommodate up to 325 passengers. While you are in Seattle, stop by and visit their art gallery which is marine oriented, and features the work of a number of the finest Northwest artists. Ledger Marine Charters, Inc. was established in 1946 by Norman Ledger who set a high standard for them to maintain. They appreciate and value their customers . . . many have become friends over the years. They look forward to having you aboard.

Hedrick, Carson & Haynie

Yacht Consultants

**6315 SEAVIEW AVENUE
SEATTLE
783-9469
HOURS: 9:00-5:00 SEVEN DAYS A WEEK,
OR BY APPOINTMENT**

Hedrick, Carson & Haynie belong in the who's who and what's what catalogue of sailing. The company is foursome of the most experienced and well-known sailors in our ever-blossoming community of yachtsmen. John Carson, Bruce Hedrick, Rich Haynie and associate Ted Allison don't harbor their knowledge; it's part of the package at HCH. When you pay them a visit you get the hint that they'd rather be sailing, but because of their dedication to the sport, they'd like to help you get out on the water . . . in the boat of your dreams, well-equipped and well-advised. HCH sells carefully selected, high quality, new and used off-shore yachts from the world's finest manufacturers, including Valiant, Espirit, Swift, Peterson, and Zap. If the sloop that is right for you is moored in the Mediterranean or off the shore of Antigua . . . the HCH crew is always prepared to go hunting for it. All boats brokered through this firm are carefully tested and inspected; the quality is thoroughly dependable. The HCH consulting service is available to their own customers as well as those who have purchased boats elsewhere. You'll receive the best available advice on equipping and preparing your vessel for long trips, making sure you have everything necessary for maximum safety and comfort. Before you sail into the sunset, visit Hedrick, Carson & Haynie first, they'll send you off in style.

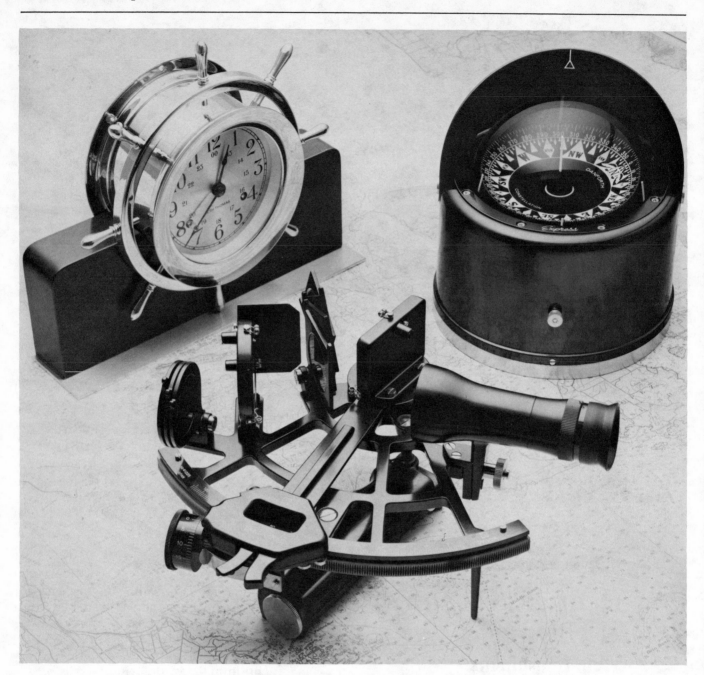

Carlsen & Larsen
Nautical Sales & Service

708 - 4TH AVENUE
622-3433
HOURS: MONDAY-FRIDAY
8:00 A.M.-5:30 P.M.
SATURDAY 9:00-1:00

Any sailor worth his salt knows that a good sailing ship is only as good as her navigational equipment. At Carlsen & Larsen Nautical Sales and Service, good sailors have been equipping their vessels with the finest accessories made, and they swear by the products and services they find here. Owners George Carlsen and Roger Larsen are experts in their field, so they not only sell nautical equipment, but provide expert maintainence and repair service as well, for everything from clocks to binoculars. Carlsen & Larsen specialize in ship's bell clocks, and feature a large selection of marine and navigation charts, compasses, and all kinds of weather instruments. Their large collection of marine related books covers a broad range of topics and includes titles of interest to everyone from novices to seasoned old salts.

Visa. Master Charge.

 ## Down East Exposures

6535 - 49TH AVENUE N.E.
523-4059
BY APPOINTMENT

Phil Fuller is a photographer with a very special interest in tall ships. When the best and most famous of them gathered at Newport, Rhode Island during the BiCentennial, Phil and his camera were situated right in the middle of the action. The result is a series of spectacular photographs capturing all the spirit and grace of these beautiful ships. A former cadet with the U.S. Coast Guard Academy, Phil has made several trans-Atlantic crossings aboard the "Eagle", one of America's own tall ships, so his vision is a very informed one. His photographs have been shown in galleries around the Northwest and featured in newspapers and magazines. Phil has found that even non-boating people appreciate his work . . . the photos make beautiful additions to offices, homes and of course well-appointed boat interiors. They come framed or matted in almost any size from 8 x 10 up to wall panels, and are priced from $25 to $250. Selections from the series are also available as a calendar as well as in a first-edition portfolio, especially for collectors.

 ## Prism
Creative Boatnames

SUITE 235, MARINERS SQUARE
1900 N. NORTHLAKE WAY
633-5848
HOURS: MONDAY - FRIDAY 8:30-4:30

Prism Creative Boatnames is a company that does just what you might imagine . . . creates and designs names for boats. The designs are applied using a special technique that outlasts ordinary paint and, with proper care, won't chip, fade or peel. It will last as long as the boat does. This unique service was started by Robert and Lynnette McPake, two graphic designers whose love for boating got the better of them. They joined up with Lee Ann Hobble and Carol Buchan and have been busy ever since. They get orders from all over the world and have designed names for trucks, cars, and airplanes as well. They execute appropriate drawings or logos to go along with the names too. Prism will apply them to the surface for a nominal charge but that's not really necessary. Once you get your Prism design, you just follow the directions and it's a piece of cake. The cost is approximately $100, which varies according to the design.

Robert H. Perry

Yacht Designers

6400 SEAVIEW AVE. N.W.
782-6633
HOURS: MONDAY-
FRIDAY 8:30-5:30

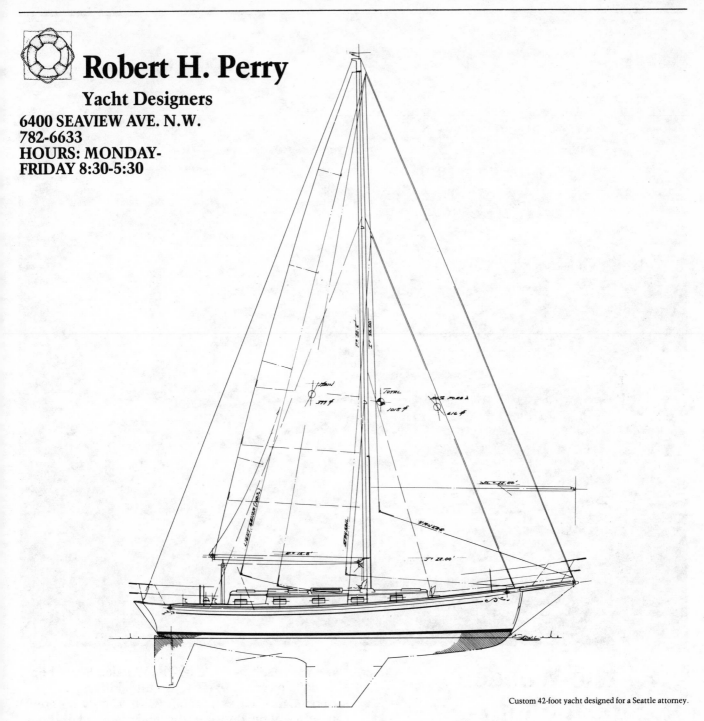

Custom 42-foot yacht designed for a Seattle attorney.

Robert H. Perry, yacht designer, has never had a burning desire to sail around the world, although that is the circumference of his fame. He doesn't dream of exotic ports. His senses come alive at his design table looking out toward Shilshole Bay. His dream, his life, is designing boats, and that's why his name is bobbing in every port, and there's not a yachting or sailing magazine that doesn't flash "Robert Perry" here or there. Perry is not dazzled by world fame, although his own yacht, the "Ricky Nelson", proudly enjoys its notoriety. It's an Esprit 37, moored a short walk away from the Perry dream factory. Bob believes that performance is paramount in every design. "You have to make it comfortable and fast, without compromise in either area." They have over 65 different designs for racers, cruisers, and family boats. These include design, for series production as well as the exotic, one-of-a-kind custom yachts. The biggest challenge and the most rewarding work for the Perry design team is working for people who know what they want and are hard to please. Some of their major clients include Valiant, Islander, Flying Dutchman, Westsail, and Nordic.

The Wooden Boat Shop

1007 N.E. BOAT STREET
634-3600
HOURS: MONDAY-FRIDAY 10:00-6:00
SATURDAY 10:00-5:00

Only a boating capital like Seattle could boast a marine supply store like The Wooden Boat Shop. An invaluable resource for owners and builders of wooden boats, this store carries supplies to fix, restore, repair and even build your own wooden boat . . . and they have all the books and manuals to show you just how to do it. The Wooden Boat Shop sells a wide variety of custom-built skiffs, small sailboats, rowboats and tenders. Or, the shop's crew can help you pick out a design and plan for building your own boat, whether for work or pleasure. Hard-to-find hardware is a specialty here. The outstanding collection includes lignum vitae, parrels, bulleyes, relaying pins, blocks and deadeyes. They also carry traditional copper and bronze hardware and fastenings, hand woodworking tools, a wide selection of books and even crawfish traps. With all this and more going for it, it's no wonder The Wooden Boat Shop is a favorite port of call for wooden boat enthusiasts. Be sure to take advantage of their mail order service.
Visa. Master Charge.

McKee & Mooney

285-1746

If you get a sudden urge to buy a nice little Swan 57 racing ketch through McKee & Mooney yacht brokers this weekend, you'll have to wait until Monday, because they'll be out sailing. The three do-or-die sailing swifts who run this luxury yacht brokering business — Henry Helliesen, Bates McKee, and Bob Mooney — not only know the sailing business, they love it. They began as a yacht maintenance service, but became enamoured with the challenge and excitement of bringing boats to Seattle that have not usually been available here. Now, they deal exclusively in buying and selling luxury sailboats . . . mostly of the Finnish Swan line, the "creme de la creme" of the cruising and racing world. Their territory from California to Alaska spans all the Northwest waters, but they've brought boats from all over the country to the Seattle market, such as the former America's Cup winner, the 12-metre sloop Weatherly. McKee & Mooney maintains an easygoing, personal approach to the business, which helps them understand which sailing vessel will be most suited to a client's needs and desires.

Yacht Systems Northwest

1800 WESTLAKE AVENUE NORTH #203
SEATTLE
283-6677
HOURS: 9:00-6:00 CLOSED TUESDAY

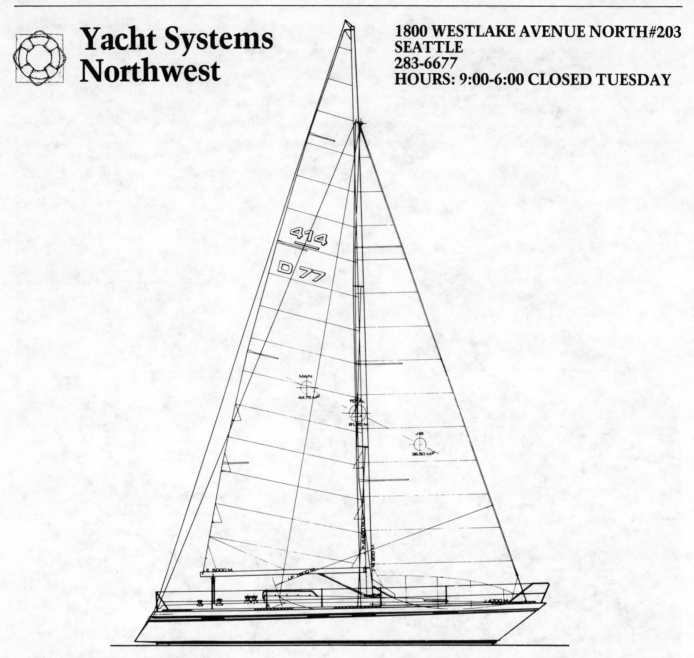

Many boat dealers will boast that they have just the dream cruiser or racing rig that you've always wanted. What they recognize at Yacht Systems Northwest is that many customers don't know what they're looking for in a yacht. So helping the customers identify their own needs and desires is a very important part of the process here. Yacht Systems Northwest has two locations. One is on the West side of Lake Union, on the water, of course, and the other is a few waves away at Winslow on Bainbridge Island. Both outlets specialize in the sale of quality racing and cruising sailboats both new and used. Customer satisfaction is the most important consideration. Repeat and referral business is the key to a successful and respected dealership and that is exactly what Yacht Systems Northwest has

established. Their goal is finding boats to provide the customer with the best service and performance. Some of the many vessels available include Yamaha sailboats from 24' to 36' feet, ranging in price from $18,000 to $90,000. Or perhaps you're interested in a Danish built 33' International 101 or Bianca 414, a luxury racer and cruiser that starts at $160,000. The salespeople at Yacht Systems Northwest are sailors who love to test performance and skill. They sponsor two annual match races. One is the Restaurateurs' Invitational Match Race. The other popular event is an invitational yacht club match race called the Bianca Cup. Yacht Systems Northwest is a fun dealership with a conviction to be involved in the Northwest yachting scene, and share that with their customers.

Leisure Time

Photo: Historical Society of Seattle & King County

The nicest winter I ever spent was a summer on Puget Sound.

Mark Twain

Chateau Ste. Michelle

**14111 N.E. 145TH STREET
WOODINVILLE, WASHINGTON 98072
(206) 488-1133
HOURS: SEVEN DAYS A WEEK 10:00-4:30
CLOSED FOR MAJOR HOLIDAYS**

Chateau Ste. Michelle is Washington's foremost producer of award-winning premium table wines. Located in Woodinville in a beautiful old-world chateau on 87 acres of wooded and cultivated land 15 miles northeast of Seattle, the winery conducts guided tours daily between 10 and 4. The wine is produced from old-world vinifera grapes grown in the Yakima Valley and Columbia River Basin, where the combination of soil, sunshine and moisture is ideal for growing wine grapes. During the tour visitors are guided step by step through the winemaking process that produces Ste. Michelle's full range of varietal wines. You'll see where the grapes arrive and follow them through crushing, fermentation, racking and filtration, and aging in oak cooperage. After the tour, guests are invited to sample several Ste. Michelle wines, and visit the Chateau wine shop which features wine, cheese, bread and fruit. If this all seems too irresistable, you can purchase picnic fixings and dine at one of the many redwood tables on the grounds.

Thomas Burke Memorial Washington State Museum

MUSEUM DB-10, UNIVERSITY OF WASHINGTON CAMPUS
543-5590
HOURS: TUESDAY-SATURDAY 10:00-4:30
THURSDAY 10:00-9:00
SUNDAY 1:00-4:30

The Thomas Burke Memorial Museum is a natural history museum with an engaging 100-year collection of anthropological, archaeological, geological and zoological specimens housed in a modern building on the University of Washington campus. If you were wondering where in Seattle the dinosaurs hang out, this is the place. There are exhibits of other fossil animals and plants, along with tools, weapons, household goods, and ritual objects from Pacific Island peoples, Northwest Coast Indians, and the western Arctic Eskimo. Shells from the Pacific Rim area and Washington State fossils and minerals are also on display. The Museum has traveling study collections and exhibits available for a small cost, a service that school teachers and recreation groups find extremely useful. Besides providing an educational and recreational resource for the museum visitor, there's a gift shop where items similar to those in the exhibits may be purchased. Northwest Coast Indian prints, cards and jewelry; Eskimo baskets and ivory carvings; dinosaur books, puzzles, T-shirts, and models; shells and rocks; and Pacific Island crafts are just a sample of what is available. The cafe surrounded by 18th century hand carved paneling is newly-opened. Coffee or tea and a pastry is a fine idea after fossil viewing.

Continuing Education at the University of Washington

LEWIS HALL
UNIVERSITY OF WASHINGTON
543-2590   543-2591
HOURS: MONDAY-
FRIDAY 8:00-5:00

Education is a continuous process, a vital part of life that no one ever outgrows. That's what Continuing Education at the University of Washington is all about. Continuing Education is entrusted with the important purpose of providing learning opportunities to people in the Puget Sound region and throughout the state . . . opportunities that enrich, challenge and even entertain students of all ages. The choice of programs is broad enough to meet a great variety of needs. Numerous credit and non-credit courses are available through the traditional classroom presentation, but many studies are offered in more unusual formats and settings. There are special conferences, workshops, seminars and correspondence courses that employ a diverse and imaginative range of community resources and communication media. Lectures & Concerts is a major program sponsored by Continuing Education. Offerings focus on cultural experiences and musical performances, many designed to appeal to the entire family. Continuing Education at the University of Washington believes that individual development, culture and education are integrally linked processes, and should be readily accessible. Continuing Education describes its activities quarterly, in a publication aptly called ''Spectrum''. Exploring a copy is a convenient way to discover the world of learning made possible by Continuing Education.

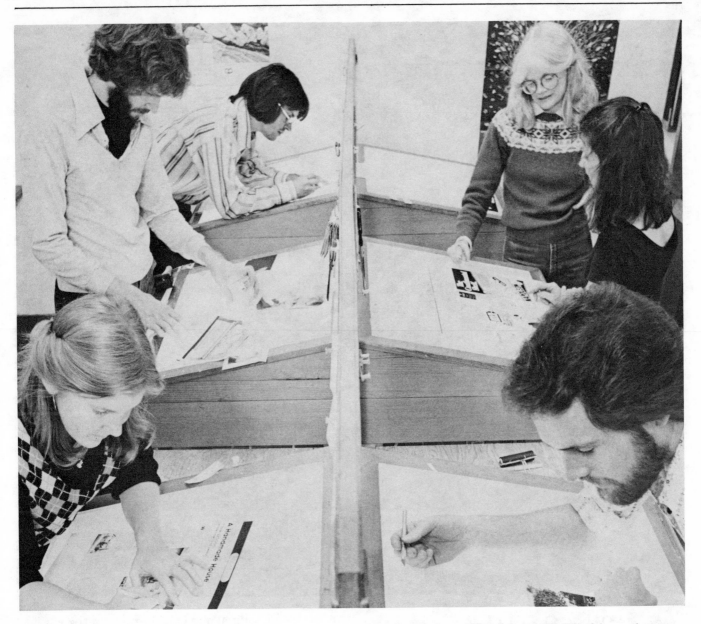

The Weekly
Seattle's Newsmagazine

85 S. WASHINGTON STREET
623-3709
HOURS: 24-HOURS-A-DAY TO ORDER A SUBSCRIPTION OR SAMPLE COPY

In just three years, the Weekly has become known as Seattle's leading newsprint magazine. Published every Wednesday, it has a following of readers who regard the paper as an essential part of their life in Seattle. Because it's published once a week, the editors and writers are free from the deadline pressures of the daily newspapers, allowing a more considered, in-depth treatment of issues, events and the people that affect them. The Weekly strikes an admirable balance between news and analysis and contains independent writing and reporting on matters of vital concern to city residents. The editorial coverage of issues, politics, places and personalities always produces interesting reading along with a thorough events calendar, news and reviews, sports and reporting from the restaurant and entertainment scene. The Weekly also publishes three companion publications: The Weekly's Reader, a monthly book review; SeattleSport, a monthly sports section of the Weekly; and the SeattleGuides, a series of seasonal quarterly guides published in two editions for Seattleites and visitors. The Weekly is available on newsstands throughout metropolitan Seattle for 50¢ a copy or by yearly subscription for $15 which is 40% less than the newsstand price.

The Seattle Aquarium

PIER 59, WATERFRONT PARK
625-5030
HOURS: SUMMER: MAY 15-SEPT. 15
DAILY 10:00 A.M.-9:00 P.M.
WINTER SEPT. 16-MAY 14
DAILY 10:00 A.M.-5:00 P.M.

When's the last time you came nose to nose with a sea otter, watched salmon swim overhead, or introduced your child to a starfish? These are just a few of the surprises waiting for you at the new Seattle Aquarium. The Aquarium is a water wonderland of intelligently-designed exhibits that are both educational and entertaining for the whole family. As you walk through a chronological panorama of the evolution of life, the sea unfolds taking you from the most primitive plant life to the warm-blooded mammals. There are creatures here of every imaginable color and variety, each one displayed in its natural habitat. Children especially enjoy the "hands-on" exhibits, where they can actually touch some of the more common shore creatures. In the spectacular underwater dome, you can watch Puget Sound sealife swim freely over, around and under you. Another spellbinding spectacle is The Aquarium water ladder, teeming with spawning salmon each year. But the real stars are the sea otters and seals — they swim, cavort and play for onlookers like born hams. Admission is $2.50 for adults, $1.25 for teenagers and seniors, and 75¢ for children age 6-12. Annual passes for individuals and families are also available.

Woodland Park Zoo

5500 PHINNEY AVENUE N.
782-1265
CALL FOR RECORDED SCHEDULE AND
CURRENT FEATURE INFORMATION.

The Woodland Zoological Park, made up of a group of naturalistic exhibits, is one of Seattle's most popular attractions. It has undergone many changes and improvements since it opened in 1904, to become one of the most beautiful, up-to-date facilities of its kind in the nation. The new Gorilla Exhibit encompasses 16,000 square feet of outdoor habitat, with streams and lush vegetation where the animals roam freely. Waterfowl and wading birds live in an environment designed to duplicate a wooded swamp. The Nocturnal House turns day into night, simulating the conditions that allow visitors to observe nocturnal animals in their most active state. The Children's Zoo is as popular with adults as it is with kids, and during summer months there is a "contact program" to acquaint children with farm animals. Guided tours are available for group by advance reservation, and illustrated self-guided tour brochures can also be purchased for a nominal fee. The best times to visit the zoo are weekdays in the early morning or late afternoon, when the animals are generally more active. Admission is $1.50 for adults and 50¢ for children, the handicapped and people over 65. The 5th day of each month is free admission day, and annual passes are available at $5 for individuals and $10 for families. Telephone the Administration Office or the Education Office at Woodland Park Zoo for more information.

Seattle Harbor Tours

PIER 56, SEATTLE, WA. 98101
FOOT OF SENECA STREET,
 1 BLOCK S. OF SEATTLE AQUARIUM
623-1445
HOURS: TOURS MAY THRU OCTOBER
MAY 1-31 — 12:15, 1:45, 3:15
JUNE 1-SEPT. 30 — 11:00, 12:15, 1:45, 3:15, 4:30
OCT. 1-31 — 12:15, 1:45, 3:15
CHARTERS YEAR AROUND
PRICES: ADULTS $3.00, CHILDREN $1.50

Longtime residents of the city discover Seattle Harbor Tours for the first time by taking out-of-town visitors on one, and then wonder why they waited so long. The fleet of 3 Goodtime tour vessels provide 5 daily tours of Elliott Bay, one of the most beautiful deep water harbors in the world; plus two trips daily to historic Tillicum Village on Blake Island for authentic Indian salmon dinners. Harbor tours last an hour and are narrated by your skipper who revises his information daily on the ships that move in and out of our busy world marine trade center. You'll also hear about Seattle's rich past, the founding of the city, the Alaska Gold Rush and our special ties with the Far East. In bright weather a Seattle Harbor Tour makes possible some of the best views of spectacular Puget Sound scenery. When it rains, you'll still enjoy the view, from the warm spacious, modern interior . . . with bar facilities, sound system and ample seating. Private parties on the Goodtime fleet are easy to arrange — for birthdays, weddings, business meetings, dinner dances and receptions. Prices for the tour are $3 for adults and $1.50 for children; rates for chartered parties can be arranged by telephone.

Longacres
Race Track

P.O. BOX 60
RENTON, WASHINGTON 98055
226-3131
Racing season: May through September
Twilight racing on weekdays. Afternoon
programs on weekends and holidays.
RESTAURANT: OPEN MONDAY-FRIDAY
FROM 11:30 A.M.
OFF SEASON: FOR LUNCH FROM 11:30 A.M.

The Sport of Kings has been a tradition for all in the Seattle area since 1933, at Longacres Race Track. For 46 years from May through September, 10 times a day, 1100 times a year, rain or shine, the thoroughbreds run at Longacres . . . making this one of the oldest sporting establishments in the area, and now, the last remaining outdoor professional sport. From the flash at the gate to the winner's circle roses, all the color, speed and drama of horse racing are viewed in style from the attractive Longacres facility. There are over 17 food concessions, from hot dog stands to elegant restaurants, plus a dozen lounges and private club rooms. Groups are welcome at Longacres, where the "Day at the Races" program includes admission, reserved group seating, the famous "all you can eat" buffet in three price choices, a tour upon request and many other extras. Tours are available every Saturday and Sunday during the season — a behind the Paddock look at horse racing conducted by former jockey Tony Perry. During the off-season, Longacres does not lock up; it's still a popular place for lunch. The Longacres Express is open Monday through Friday from 11 to 4. For information on group rates and any other questions, call the information office.
Visa. Master Charge.

Lake Quinault Lodge

**P.O. BOX 7
QUINAULT, WASHINGTON 98575
INFORMATION: 288-2571
TOLL FREE IN WASHINGTON:
1-800-562-6672**

Sometimes the best thing about a city is getting out of it. But, where to go? Not a hiker, distance cyclist, Hawaii a little beyond the budget, and a tent wasn't what you had in mind. You should know about Lake Quinault Lodge, a nationally famous, magnificent wilderness resort, situated on the shores of the picturesque lake for which it is named . . . in the heart of the Olympic National Forest. This ideal get-away was built 50 years ago and its authentic period decor has been updated with all the comforting conveniences and resort necessities, like an indoor pool, sauna, and commodious beautifully appointed rooms. Some of the rooms have balconies from which to view the lake and ponder which of the recreational alternatives to opt for . . . boating, canoeing, swimming, hunting, fishing, or maybe just a leisurely promenade around the lake and its surrounding natural beauty. What these activities have in common, of course, is the appetite they'll create, which may be delightfully accommodated by the gourmet fare in the Lodge's dining room. Open year-round, Lake Quinault Lodge has excellent convention facilities for up to 110 people. Mid-week visits are especially nice; the rates are lower and the selection of rooms are a little wider. In any case, reservations should be made if you'd like to visit this popular place.

Kalaloch Lodge

**BOX 1100, STAR ROUTE 1
KALALOCH, WASHINGTON 98331
(206) 962-2271**

Northwest marine air, beautiful scenery and relaxation as you want.

If it occurs that you haven't retreated from those urban pressures for rather too long, what could be better to revive you than a dose of ocean air? Kalaloch Lodge on the western reaches of the Olympic Peninsula has as spectacular a view of the Pacific as you could hope to abandon yourself to. Kalaloch welcomes you with a choice of settings . . . the spacious rooms in the Lodge itself or the new Sea Crest House . . . or a secluded cabin where you're on your own with cooking appliances, and a unique ocean vantage point. The recreation available is strictly the mellowest, and probably just what the doctor ordered . . . go beachcombing and hunt for driftwood and Japanese glass floats; rent a shovel and dig up some razor clams, go stream-fishing, or explore the moss-hung rainforests in this ocean strip of the Olympic National Park. Reservations to go to the Kalaloch Lodge should be arranged in advance, but once you're there, there are many services available, through the dining room, coffee shop, cocktail lounge, store and gas station . . . assurance that your only concern is taking in as much bracing

The Captain Whidbey Inn
on Whidbey Island

COUPEVILLE, WASHINGTON
(206) 678-4097
PLEASE CALL AHEAD FOR RESERVATIONS.

The Captain Whidbey Inn is really special — it's like running away from home but it only takes 90 minutes. Ideally, you'll want to stay for a few days, but even if you can only get away from it all for an evening, this is the place to go for dinner. Built in 1907, the Inn retains all the turn-of-the-century atmosphere that first made it popular, back in the days when paddlewheel steamboats delivered guests from Seattle and Tacoma right up to the dock. The rooms at the Inn are rustic and charming, many furnished with antiques. Some rooms have verandas overlooking two lagoons and Penn Cove, and others are all on their own in small cottages scattered over the spacious grounds. The dining room offers a fine menu, featuring seafood and an excellent wine list, and after dinner you can enjoy all the other pleasures of a country inn: the Chart Room for after-dinner drinks and romantic view, a well-stocked library, and comfortable sitting room. The best time to visit is during the week, when there are fewer people and the relaxing atmosphere is at its best.
Visa. BankAmericard.

Pacific Science Center

**200 2ND AVENUE N.
AT SEATTLE CENTER
625-9333
24-HOUR INFORMATION LINE: 382-2887**

The lofty white arches at the Seattle Center landmark this beautiful facility where science is fun and fascinating, not dry and confusing. The Pacific Science Center is a non-profit educational foundation dedicated to promoting better understanding of science and technology. The center is filled with stimulating "hands-on" exhibits that have been popular with countless children and adults ever since it opened at the Seattle World's Fair in 1962. There's something for everyone . . . a volcano watch, computer works, math puzzles, a planetarium, dazzling Imax 70 mm. films and other multi-media presentations . . . and traveling exhibits brought in from all over the world. The "Arches" giftshop at the Pacific Science Center is not to be overlooked either. It has one of the most intriguing collections of games, toys, crafts, and books about every subject you can or can't think of. Admission to the Pacific Science Center is $2.50 for adults, and $1.00 for those under 17 or over 65.

Kingdome Tours

**GATE D,
THE KINGDOME
201 S. KING STREET
628-3331 628-3383
HOURS: 11:00 AM, 1:00 PM,
and 3:00 PM
DAILY, EXCEPT WHEN
SUSPENDED DUE
TO EVENT.**

Although it is still a relatively recent addition to the scenery, the Kingdome has become an authentic Seattle landmark. Owned and built by King County taxpayers, it is the only super-stadium in the country to operate in the black its first year. It plays host to four major league sports teams as well as dozens of other entertaining events each year. The Kingdome Tours program offers a 45-minute backstage look at the daily operations of this mammoth structure. Guides explain the history of the Kingdome and take you through areas not normally open to the public, like locker rooms, press areas and the playing field. Even if you've attended Kingdome events many times, the tour is well worth your while, because it offers a perspective you won't have seen before. The cost is $1.50 for adults and teenagers, and 75¢ for children aged 6 - 12 and seniors over 65. Call the Kingdome to confirm tour times.

The Seattle Center

305 HARRISON ST.
625-4234

In 1962, Seattle hosted Century 21, the first financially successful World's Fair in history. The legacy it left behind provided Seattle with two of its most famous landmarks: The Space Needle and the Monorail. The Seattle Center, a beautiful 74-acre urban park, is still one of the city's premier attractions for residents and visitors. The Center has many faces, and its variety of attractions have no rival anywhere in the country. A hub for performing arts, The Center offers opera, symphony, dance, theatre, and festivals year round which take place in the Playhouse, Opera House, and throughout the entire Center grounds. Each year is highlighted with major festivals — Science Fiction Expo, Imagination Celebration, the Northwest Regional Folk Life Festival, and Bumbershoot — along with countless ethnic and holiday celebrations. The Center is popular for conventions and meetings, with facilities to accommodate every activity from a small committee meeting to a major national convention. The Coliseum, Arena, and Memorial Stadium are choice facilities for spectator sports. It's also an arts and crafts center with two major galleries, an amusement park, retail outlets and a wide range of food services. The Seattle Center is a beautiful urban park where you can spend the day, enjoy the scenery, fountains and attractions, and never spend a dime. This park belongs to the city. In many ways, it *is* the city and has a lot to do with Seattle's status as the most livable city in the country.

Index